GALATIANS
AND
EPHESIANS

LESSONS IN LIFE AND LIBERTY

Light to My Path Series

Old Testament

Ezra, Nehemiah, and Esther
Job
Isaiah
Jeremiah and Lamentations
Ezekiel
· *Daniel, Hosea, and Joel*
Amos, Obadiah, and Jonah
Micah, Nahum, Habakkuk, and Zephaniah
Haggai, Zechariah, and Malachi

New Testament

John
Acts
Romans
1 Corinthians
2 Corinthians
Galatians and Ephesians
Philippians and Colossians
James and 1 & 2 Peter
The Epistles of John and Jude

Galatians
and
Ephesians

Lessons in Life and Liberty

F. Wayne Mac Leod

Authentic

Authentic Publishing
We welcome your questions and comments.

USA   PO Box 444, 285 Lynnwood Ave, Tyrone, GA, 30290
         authentic@stl.org or www.authenticbooks.com
UK   9 Holdom Avenue, Bletchley, Milton Keynes, Bucks, MK1 1QR, UK
         www.authenticmedia.co.uk
India   Logos Bhavan, Medchal Road, Jeedimetla Village,
         Secunderabad 500 055, A.P.

Galatians and Ephesians
ISBN-10: 1-932805-74-5
ISBN-13: 978-1-932805-74-1

Cover design: Paul Lewis
Interior design: Angela Lewis
Editorial team: Bette Smythe KJ James, Dana Bromley

Printed and bound in India by
OM Authentic Media, P.O.Box 2190, Secunderabad 500 003
E-mail: printing@ombooks.org

Contents

Ephesians

Preface

In the book of Galatians, the apostle Paul spoke to the believers of his day about the place of the law of Moses in their newly established relationship with the Lord Jesus. He took a firm stand against a gospel of law but strongly supported the gospel of salvation by faith in Jesus Christ alone. He reminded the Galatians that through the work of the Lord Jesus, they were set free from the law and its requirements and were adopted as sons and daughters of God.

In the book of Ephesians, the apostle reminded believers of their position and benefits in the Lord Jesus. He offered them some guidelines for walking in the Spirit and showed them how to prepare for the spiritual battle that each of them would face. He also taught some principles on dealing with family and work relationships.

As with all the books in this series, my desire is that you read the Bible passage along with this commentary. If you only read this commentary, you are missing a vital part of what I am trying to accomplish. This commentary is *not* a replacement for the Bible. It is merely a study aid. I encourage you to read it along with the Scripture passage listed at the beginning of each chapter. This book is not a replacement for the Holy Spirit either. While I trust that the Spirit of God has led me in the writing of this work, I recognize that he must also lead you in the reading and study of it and the Scripture it is meant to explain. Ask the Spirit of God to give you insight. He may choose to use this commentary to give you that insight, or he may challenge you directly. What is important is that you let the Spirit of God guide you in your study.

As you begin would you take a moment to bring a few matters to the Lord? First, please pray that God would use this work in your life to draw you closer to him. Second, please pray that God would bless this book in the lives of others around the world. Literally thousands of copies of books in this series are being sent to needy pastors and Christian workers around the world. Please join me in prayer that this book and others in the series will be useful tools in the hands of God's Spirit to bring many closer to Christ.

May God richly bless you as you embark on this study.

F. Wayne Mac Leod

Galatians

1

Another Gospel

Read Galatians 1:1–10

This is a letter written to the churches in Galatia, a region of Asia Minor (modern Turkey). The letter was not written to any particular church but to a group of churches in this general area. Paul had established churches in some southern Galatian cities on his first missionary journey (Acts 13:14–14:23). Paul later wrote to these churches to confront a very particular problem—the temptation to return to the law of Moses and see it as a means of salvation and the evidence of a Spirit-filled life.

In verse 1 Paul introduced himself as an apostle ("sent one"). The role of apostle was a very particular one in the early church. God had chosen these individuals to lay the foundation of his church on earth. Notice that Paul reminded the Galatians that his calling to be an apostle was not from men. He was called by God to exercise this role. Notice, more precisely, that the apostle was called by Jesus Christ and God the Father who raised him from the dead. The resurrected Jesus had personally appeared to Paul and called him as an apostle (Acts 9:1–9, 15).

Without the gracious work of Jesus Christ, Paul's calling would have been meaningless. Without the death of the Lord Jesus on his behalf, Paul, like each of us, would have been destined to an eternity of separation from God. His death and resurrection conquered sin and the grave for us. Paul's hope and message were focused on this redeeming work of the Lord Jesus.

Paul sent greetings and concern from the brothers who were with him. We are not told who these friends were, but they shared Paul's concern about the welfare of the churches in Galatia.

In verse 3 Paul sent his wishes for God's grace and peace to the churches in Galatia. Grace is God's unmerited favor. Paul's desire was that the undeserved favor of God rest on the Galatian believers. The peace Paul desired for the churches comes from a right relationship with the Lord Jesus. Only when people have been forgiven and brought into a right relationship with the Father is this peace established. Paul's desire for the Galatians was that they know and enjoy the full blessings of God as his beloved children.

The person of the Lord Jesus is central to Paul's introduction to this book. In verse 4 Paul reminded his readers that it was the Lord Jesus who gave himself for their sins. Jesus willingly died on the horrible cross of Calvary for them. He suffered the insults of those he created. He willingly endured the pain and suffering inflicted on him. Why did he do this? Paul stated here that Jesus did this to deliver believers from the present evil age.

What is this evil age? This age began when Adam, the first man, opened the door for sin to enter the world. God's curse fell, and all creation was destined to be eternally separated from God and under his divine wrath. The physical world and every living thing began to suffer and decay. Old age and its effects became a constant reminder that no one would escape the jaws of death. Also, there was the breaking down of social relationships. Adam's own son murdered his brother. The disruption of marriages, the disrespect for authority, crime, violence, and all the world's corrupt systems became characteristics of this evil age.

However, according to the will of the Father, the death of Jesus on the cross of Calvary broke the curse of sin and brought salvation to all who would believe in him. The very thought of the full sacrifice of the Lord Jesus Christ stirred Paul to the very core of his being: "To whom be glory for ever and ever. Amen" (verse 5). Could there ever be anything more wonderful than this? I am set free from the curse. All my sins are forgiven. I am rescued from the power of the devil and this world's corruptions. I will enjoy worship and friendship with God for eternity. And it is all because of Jesus and what he has done for me.

It is in this context that Paul stated in verse 6 that he marveled that the Galatians had turned so soon from the Lord Jesus and the freedom and hope they had in him. The Greek word translated as "astonished" is a very strong word. It has the idea of this: "I cannot believe that you would ever turn from the grace that you have. What you have done defies all understanding. No person in his or her right mind would ever do what you have done."

According to Paul, the Galatians had turned away from the true gospel ("good news") of grace to a legalistic belief. How had this happened? There were false teachers and prophets among them who had convinced them against the clear teaching of the apostles. These wicked individuals distorted and perverted the gospel of Christ. How had they done this? Paul answered this question throughout the remainder of this letter. In brief, however, they had been teaching that a believer needed to be circumcised and observe the laws of Moses in order to be saved and enjoy the favor of God. This, according to Paul, was a perversion of the gracious gospel of Christ. We shall examine this in greater detail throughout the course of this study.

Notice in verses 8 and 9 how strongly Paul felt about the perversion of the gospel by adding the requirements of the law. Paul told the Galatians that even if an apostle or an angel from heaven were to preach this perverted message of the gospel, he would be eternally cursed! This is a very strong statement. Who among us would have the courage to curse an angel of God or one of the apostles? There is anger in Paul's words. This anger is directed toward anyone who would diminish the importance of the finished work of Christ on the cross for our sins. Christ's work alone is sufficient for salvation. Nothing more can be added. To say that the Galatians needed the law to merit God's favor and salvation was to say that Christ did not do enough. Anyone who depreciated the work of Christ for the salvation of humanity needed to be dealt with in the strictest manner.

Paul did not care what anyone else thought about his views on this matter (verse 10). He was not looking for the approval of the Galatians. He was willing to risk his relationship with them for the sake of the truth. As an apostle, his role was to guard the truth that Christ had passed on to him. Paul was willing to do this even if it meant losing friends. If he was trying to please men, he could not be a servant of God. There was a choice to be made. Would he please God and stand up for the truth, or would he please the Galatians and let them continue in their error? Paul chose to please God.

For Consideration:

- What things do we add to the gospel in our day? Can we be guilty of preaching another gospel?

- Why are people attracted to a message that says that we need to do this or that to gain the approval of God?

- Why is it so hard for us to accept the fact that the work of Jesus Christ alone is sufficient to save us from our sins?

For Prayer:

- Thank the Lord that there is nothing more to be done for our salvation except to surrender and accept what he has already accomplished on the cross.

- Thank the Lord that he accepts you just as you are without having to do anything to gain his favor.

- Do you know someone who is caught up in the teaching of another gospel? Take a moment to pray that the Lord would reveal to this person the sufficiency of his work alone.

2

The Revelation of the Gospel to Paul

Read Galatians 1:11–24

In the last meditation, we saw how strongly Paul felt about the perversion of the message of the gospel. The gospel had become his passion in life. Paul's life was devoted to the proclamation of the message that Jesus died for our sins and rose victorious over sin and death. This truth had radically changed his life. As he preached it to others, they too were transformed by the power of that message. Here in this next section, Paul shed some light on how he came to understand this message that had so radically transformed his life.

Paul wanted the Galatians to realize that the message of the gospel did not come to him by human teaching. It was not a human idea or philosophy passed on through the ages. The gospel had its origin in God himself. The gospel ("good news") is the wonderful plan of God for the salvation of his people.

Paul stated in verses 12–16 that he had not come to understand the message of the gospel through men. The reality of the matter was that the more men had spoken to him about the gospel, the more he had reacted against it. He had wanted nothing to do with this teaching. Verse 13 tells us that Paul had once hated anything to do with the message of Christ. He had lashed out in intense persecution against anyone who accepted this teaching, which he considered heretical to the Judaism he so zealously practiced.

The book of Acts tells the story of how Paul (here called Saul) was on his way to Damascus to persecute the church (Acts 9). On the way he was stopped by a great light coming down from heaven, and a voice spoke out of that light. The voice was that of the Lord Jesus, speaking and revealing himself to Paul. This encounter with the Lord he had been persecuting transformed Paul's life. Never again would he be the same. Never would he forget the words he heard that day. His eyes and ears were opened. His heart was touched. From that point onward, he would proclaim with deep conviction that the gospel he had so intensely rejected was not only the truth but the only hope of salvation from the flames of eternal hell.

What was it about Paul's experience that made such an impact? He had no doubt heard the message of the gospel prior to this, but it had not changed his life. But this time God himself revealed the message to Paul and this transformed his life and thinking. Ultimately, this is what has to happen to each of us. God must reveal himself to each of us personally. While you may have heard the message through human lips, it is only as the Sovereign God himself speaks directly to your soul through his Holy Spirit that you will ever truly come to understand and accept the claims of the gospel.

Notice in verse 15 that God had his hand on Paul from his birth. Even through the time when Paul persecuted the church, God was working in the life of this man. Outwardly, there was no clear, visible evidence that God was going to bring him to salvation, but from the very beginning of time, God had a specific purpose for Paul. In time that plan was revealed to him.

Verse 16 is very important. Notice how Paul said that God was pleased to reveal his Son "in" him. There is a world of difference between the word "in" and the word "to." There are many people *to* whom Christ is revealed. These people have an understanding of his work. They can tell you who Jesus is and what he came to accomplish on this earth. Christ has not been revealed *in* them, however. When Christ is revealed to us, we understand intellectually who he is and what he came to do. When Christ is revealed in us, however, he comes to take up residence in our lives for the purpose of transforming us. His presence empowers us. We speak of Christ not as someone we have heard and read about but as someone we know personally. When Christ is revealed in us, his power and wisdom become part of us. His life flows through us. There is a radical change that takes place.

Paul tells us in 2 Corinthians 5:17 that if anyone is *in* Christ, he is a new creation. Paul was so passionate about the message of the gospel because he was experiencing it personally in his life. Paul's understanding of the gospel did not come to him by human means but by a very special revelation of God to him personally. Has God revealed himself to you in this manner?

Paul went on in verse 16 to remind his readers that even after his conversion to Christ, he did not consult men. Paul's understanding of the gospel did not come about as a result of human teaching either before his conversion or after his conversion. He makes it clear to us here that after his conversion he did not consult with the other apostles in Jerusalem but went into Arabia. There he was removed from those who belonged to the Lord. As a new believer, all he had was God and his Word. He was not trained by men to believe a certain way. Only after three years did Paul go to meet with Peter (with whom he stayed for fifteen days). During that time he never saw any of the other apostles except James, the brother of the Lord Jesus (verse 19).

Why does Paul tell us these things and what implications do they have for us today? Paul is telling us that the things he preached were not mere gems of human wisdom. What he preached was the wisdom of God revealed to him directly by God.

What does this passage have to say to us today? What does it have to say about discipleship of new believers? Should new believers be tossed out on their own to learn for themselves like Paul? Should they spend the first few years of their Christian experience in isolation from other believers? We would all agree that this would not only be foolish but also dangerous for a new believer. Satan is only too willing to distort and take away the little truth a new believer has.

How are we to understand Paul's actions here? It seems to me that the key is for us to understand that it is more important for the new believer to be able to hear from God than it is for them to hear from us. All too often new believers become clones of those who disciple them. In discipling others, we often push our denominational and theological systems. We are sometimes tempted to show the new believer why we are right and why others are wrong. We train them to think as we do, to worship as we do, and to associate with people just like us. New believers hear from us, but do they learn to hear from God? When we have finished taking them through our discipleship program, who have they learned from? Have we given them the right to differ from us in their understanding of the Scriptures? Are we leading them to become what God wants them to become, or are we encouraging them to become what we think they need to become? Are we leading them to have personal convictions, or are we simply handing them our own beliefs?

The years following Paul's conversion were years of hearing from God directly. In those years personal convictions were formed. These convictions were not secondhand truths passed on to him from other believers. Secondhand convictions do not create passion for service. Many believers remain weak in faith because of their weak convictions.

Paul's passion in ministry came as a result of his deeply felt, personal beliefs. The living Christ was real to Paul because he was being revealed *in* Paul. The resurrected Christ was revealing his gospel of truth to Paul so he could preach Christ among the Gentiles. The result was that people saw the difference in

Paul's life. They glorified God because of what they saw God doing in the life of this former persecutor of the church.

For Consideration:

- Has Christ been revealed in you? What are the evidences of this in your life?

- Are the convictions you have your own personal convictions? Do you believe what you believe because you are convinced before God after personal study and reflection or because someone else told you that this is what is right to believe?

- Is there a difference between preaching personal convictions and preaching secondhand convictions? What is the difference?

For Prayer:

- Thank God that he has revealed the gospel to you personally.

- Thank God that he had his hand on you long before you came to a personal knowledge of the salvation he offers.

- Do you know someone who, like Paul, is running from the truth? Take a moment to pray that God would reveal himself to this person.

3

The Apostle to the Gentiles

Read Galatians 2:1–10

While it is clear that God himself had revealed the message of the gospel to Paul, it took a certain time for him to be accepted in the Christian community. Initially, even the other apostles had trouble accepting that this great persecutor of the church had become a true believer. This hesitation on the part of the church was further complicated by the fact that Paul's particular burden was to preach this gospel to the Gentile community and not exclusively to the Jews, as was the tendency of the day.

Here in this section of his letter, Paul explained how his ministry came to be accepted by the other apostles. He began by saying that after fourteen years he went up to Jerusalem with Barnabas and Titus. We are not sure of the exact timing of this trip to Jerusalem. Some see it as being fourteen years after his conversion, but the timing is not important. What is important is the reason for his trip to Jerusalem. Verse 2 states that he went in response to a revelation from God and to set before the church in Jerusalem the gospel he preached to the Gentiles. In other words, he went to give an account of his actions and the message he was preaching to the non-Jewish community.

It should be understood here that there were two principle barriers Paul had to overcome in his preaching to the Gentiles. First, there was the fact that for so long the Gentile community was seen as being separate from God's overall plan of salvation. Initially, Jesus told the disciples to take his message to the house of Israel (Matthew 10:5–7). Even in the early church, evangelism was preached primarily only to the Jewish community (Acts 11:19). In preaching to the Gentiles, Paul was going against tradition.

The second problem Paul had to deal with was the place of the Jewish law in the lives of the Gentile converts. While there were some Jewish believers who were willing to see the Gentiles come to know the Lord, they still believed that Gentiles were required to live according to the law of Moses. Jews expected that a male Gentile who was converted to Christ be circumcised and follow other Jewish religious traditions. Some Jews even made this a requirement for salvation for the Gentile. We have already seen in the first chapter that Paul formally rejected this doctrine. He believed that all people are saved by grace, that is, without practicing the law of Moses. Here again Paul went against strong tradition.

Notice in verse 2 that Paul went to Jerusalem because of a revelation from God. We are not told when this occurred or how he received this revelation. However, it was the purpose of God for Paul to tell the church in Jerusalem his convictions on the matter of God's plan for the Gentiles. The church of Jerusalem had been resistant to preaching to the Gentiles, and Paul, being led of God, went to Jerusalem to speak to the church about this issue.

It is important for us to note Paul's approach. Paul went in response to a revelation from God. Despite this fact, however, Paul was very careful about how he approached the church on this issue. He could have come with a very negative attitude and publicly reprimanded the Jerusalem church. He could have come with a "God told me so" attitude. Notice, however, in verse 2 that he spoke privately to the leaders. He did so with a certain fear in his heart that he had run his race "in vain." We need to examine this attitude of Paul more closely.

How often have we been repelled by individuals who came to us with a "God told me so" attitude? Some individuals do not demonstrate wisdom and discernment in how to communicate the message God has given them. Paul spoke here with gentleness and humility. While he had a deep conviction on the matter of his calling, he wanted unity in the church. Paul had committed his life to preaching the message of grace in the gospel of Christ. He needed the Jerusalem church to support his efforts to reach out to the Gentiles and bring them into the church as equal in standing to Jewish believers. He also sought unity among the apostles on the matter of eliminating Mosaic legalism from Christianity. If God's plan was that Paul preach grace to the Gentiles, then, if the church was sensitive to the leading of the Holy Spirit, they would recognize this burden in him as being from God and support him in it. Paul did not want the church to split over the matter of Gentile converts. He placed his whole ministry before the church for their affirmation of unity and equality of all believers and a rejection of legalism. He did not want to see his efforts among the Gentiles erupt in conflict among the apostles. This was truly a humble step of faith. Would they support him or reject him and his burden?

From verses 3–5 we understand that the decision of the Jerusalem church to stand behind the message and ministry of the apostle Paul did not come easily. Titus, a Gentile who was with Paul, had been the source of certain opposition. Some Jews pressed for him to be circumcised. Paul called these individuals "false brothers" who were sent as spies. In other words, these men secretly came to discover whether Titus had been circumcised.

Paul refused to give in to the pressure of these false teachers. While there were times when the apostle did permit circumcision for the purpose of greater ministry (Acts 16:1–2), this was not one of those times. To give way to these counterfeit Christians would be to say that obedience to the Mosaic law was necessary for salvation. This was what Paul was fighting against. Obviously, his insistence paid off in the end. Verse 3 tells us that Titus was not compelled to be circumcised. He was accepted just as he was—an uncircumcised Gentile brother in Christ. What joy this must have given Paul.

In verses 6–7 Paul told his readers that the leaders in the church in Jerusalem ("those who seemed to be important") added nothing to his message. What was his message? It was that the Gentile could be saved without practicing the law of Moses. In the end, even the Jerusalem leaders accepted this message without adding any further requirements. They confirmed Paul as an apostle to the Gentiles and stood behind his message of salvation to the Gentiles without the law. Even as God had used Peter to preach the gospel to the Jews, God had been using Paul to preach to the Gentiles. Having confirmed his apostolic ministry and gospel message of grace, the apostles in Jerusalem extended to Paul and Barnabas the "right hand of fellowship," sending them out to the Gentiles with their whole-hearted approval, challenging them also to remember the poor (verses 9–10).

For Paul, nothing could be added to the message of salvation by faith in Christ alone. Humans are saved by the grace of God with no effort on their part except to believe, by God's grace, what has already been done. To place any additional requirement on anyone would be to depreciate the work of Christ. Paul's insistence in this matter caused the early church to deal with their false notions of salvation plus the law. The work of Christ alone was sufficient for salvation. Paul was very influential in bringing the church into line with the heart of the Lord Jesus for missions to the Gentile world.

For Consideration:

- Can we be guilty of presenting a message of salvation through Christ plus works? What requirements are often put on unbelievers today for their salvation?

- Have you ever found yourself seeking to merit the favor of God by your good works? Does God love you more when you serve him faithfully?

- Have you ever found yourself hesitating to accept that a person truly belonged to the Lord because he or she went to a church that did not believe the same things you believe? Could it be possible that we too are guilty of the same sin as the Jerusalem church?

- Paul had a very clear call of God to challenge the church of Jerusalem about this issue of salvation through Christ plus the law of Moses. The church of his day was not walking in line with the heart of God. Despite his conviction, how did Paul approach the church?

- Are there areas where the church of your region is not in tune with the clear heart of God? What are those areas? What needs to be done to bring the church to that humble place of sharing the heart of God?

For Prayer:

- Ask God to reveal to you any prejudice you might have against a brother or sister in Christ who does not believe or see things the way you do.

- Ask the Lord God to bring your church in line with his heart.

- Ask God to give you grace to be humble as Paul was when he dealt with this very delicate matter of unity in the church.

- Do you know some brothers or sisters who are part of a church where the gospel of salvation through Christ alone is not being clearly preached? Take a moment to pray for them and their witness in that community.

4

Paul versus Peter

Read Galatians 2:11–21

P aul's concern to see Gentile believers equally integrated into the church alongside Jewish believers brought him into conflict with the Jewish leadership. We saw in the last meditation how he defended this vision before the church in Jerusalem. While the church in Jerusalem confirmed him in his ministry, it was not easy for the leaders to change their deeply rooted Mosaic practices and mindset. Paul was even forced to reprimand the great apostle Peter for his hypocrisy.

Before we examine the conflict between Peter and Paul in Antioch, it is helpful for us to understand the background. First, the church in Antioch had a history of struggle with the differences between Jews and Gentiles. When this church began, it was the custom of the Jewish Christians to preach the gospel only to the Jews (Acts 11:19). However, God moved some believers from Cyrene and Cyprus to share the gospel also with the Gentiles in the region. This led to a major move of God's Spirit among the Gentiles and the planting of the church in Antioch.

This church seemed to be able to function for some time with both Jews and Gentiles worshiping side by side. This may have been one of the reasons for the blessing of the Lord on this particular church. These believers were learning to put aside generations of prejudice and accept each other as equal brothers and sisters in Christ. In Acts 15 false preachers came to Antioch preaching that for Gentiles to be saved, they needed to observe the law of Moses. This led to a major controversy in the church. Paul was sent to Jerusalem from Antioch to resolve this conflict. The result was that the church in Jerusalem decreed that salvation had nothing to do with the law of Moses. Salvation for Jews and Gentiles was by faith alone in Christ alone and apart from obeying the law.

When Peter came to Antioch, however, he was influenced by some individuals sent by James who taught this false notion that Gentile believers were inferior to Jewish believers because they did not practice the law of Moses. Before hearing from these individuals, Peter had been eating with Gentiles and accepting them as equal brothers in Christ. He was intimidated, however, by the false teachers and began to separate himself from the Gentile believers (verse 12). Peter had a tendency to compromise his convictions under pressure (Matthew 16:21–23; Mark 14:66–72).

Because of Peter's high profile in the believing community, he influenced many people to follow his ways. Even Barnabas began to separate himself from Gentile believers. It grieved Paul to see this perversion of the gospel and disruption of unity. Peter knew that God had accepted the Gentiles as equal partners in salvation. He knew that salvation was not through the law of Moses, but he was not living this out in his life.

It is one thing to say that we believe we are saved by our belief in Jesus alone, but how often do we put other obligations on new converts? We tell them what they have to believe, how they need to live, and who they need to associate with if they are going to be accepted as fellow believers in Christ.

Paul's life was dedicated to seeing the Gentiles accept the

message of salvation and be integrated into the church. Peter's refusal to sit with the Gentiles angered Paul because it was inconsistent with the truth. Paul did not hesitate to reprimand Peter "to his face" and "in front of them all" over this issue (verses 12, 14). Because the offense was done in public, the rebuke was done in public also.

Paul's argument here is very important. He began by reminding Peter of his inconsistency. "You are a Jew," Paul said, "yet you live like a Gentile." What was he telling Peter here? He was reminding Peter that though he was Jewish by birth, he did not live according to the ceremonial and dietary laws of the Jews. He had been set free by Christ from all these rules and regulations (Mark 7:18–19; Acts 10:9–22). While Peter did not live like a Jew himself, he was imposing Jewish customs on the Gentiles. He was demanding that they eat separately from the Jew.

Not only was Peter's lifestyle inconsistent with the truth, but he also was encouraging false teachers and false doctrine. Peter knew in his heart, as did all the other apostles, that salvation had nothing to do with the law of Moses, that no one could be saved by observing the law of Moses, and that salvation was only through the work of the Lord Jesus on the cross. "A man is not justified by observing the law, but by faith in Jesus Christ" (verse 16). To be justified means to be righteous or innocent before God. Through faith in Christ, believers are given as a free gift the righteousness of God (2 Corinthians 5:21). Peter's insistence that the Gentiles observe the law of Moses led to a false understanding of what it meant to be justified.

It is important to remember that you can appear to do all the right things, go to the right church, read your Bible, and outwardly conform to all it says and still not go to heaven. Salvation has nothing to do with what you do or don't do. It has everything to do with what the Lord Jesus did on your behalf and your acceptance and total confidence in his work alone for your right standing before God.

One of the fears of those who promoted keeping the law

of Moses was that if people were free from these commands, there would be no incentive to live godly lives. They believed that freedom from the law would encourage sinful and undisciplined lives among believers. For this reason, they insisted on salvation plus the observance of the Mosaic law.

Paul challenged this belief. If Christ came to offer a salvation without the law, does that mean that Christ is a promoter of sin (verse 17)? Paul strongly rejected this idea: "Absolutely not!" On the contrary, Christ came to offer us victory over sin—something the law could not do. He came to change us from within. The law could not change the sinful human heart but only reveal it.

All who come to Christ abandon the idea of salvation by keeping the law. In this sense, they die to the law (verse 19). Christians, according to Paul, are those who have died to all human effort to please God. They know that they are hopeless sinners in need of God's mercy and grace. The Mosaic law was never intended as a means of salvation, which has always been by repentance and faith (Psalm 51:14–17; Habakkuk 2:4). The law simply served as a mirror to reveal sin in the human heart and show the need for a savior who could change sinful hearts. This is exactly what the Lord Jesus came to do.

Paul experienced this change in his own life: "I have been crucified with Christ and I no longer live, but Christ lives in me. The life I live in the body, I live by faith in the Son of God, who loved me and gave himself for me" (verse 20). Paul was aware of a new life pulsating through his veins. It was the life of Christ. As he cooperated with this new life in him, Paul experienced wisdom and power to live a life of obedience. He became a vessel in which the Spirit of Christ lived. His constant desire for sin was broken. He proclaimed that he could do all things through Christ who was his strength (Philippians 4:13). His new life in Christ was very different from his former life in Mosaic legalism. Paul lived by faith in what the Lord Jesus had done and was doing in him. Whereas, in the past, his trust had been in what he could do for God.

Paul reminded Peter in verse 18 of the foolishness of rebuilding what had been torn down. After experiencing the power and freedom of Christ's life, how could anyone return to the futility of a former life? It was unthinkable for Paul that a believer who knew the grace of true righteousness should even desire to return to a religion of ineffective human effort.

What Paul taught here is of utmost importance if we are to understand what the Christian life is all about. Too many of us have gotten caught up in a religion of works. We try to do all the right things. We believe and teach all the right doctrines, but we are empty. Paul teaches us that the secret of the Christian life is to allow Christ to live his life in us and through us. Here and here alone is victory and true righteousness and peace. "If righteousness could be gained through the law, Christ died for nothing!" (verse 21).

For Consideration:

* Do we promote a gospel that requires obedience to rules? What are some of these rules?

* What things cause divisions in the church today? Can you accept as a true believer in Christ a brother or sister who differs from you?

* Take a moment to consider what Paul teaches here about Christ living in believers. How much of your faith consists of human effort to please God?

* What is the difference between human effort to please God and Christ living his life in you?

For Prayer:

* Ask God to reveal to you those areas of your life where you are seeking to live and serve him from your own human effort. Surrender these areas of your life to him.

- Ask the Lord to forgive you for the times when you really believed that you could please him by your own efforts.

- Thank the Lord that he accepts you just as you are. Thank him that he has done all the work necessary for your salvation.

- Ask the Lord to help you to accept a brother or sister who differs from you. Thank him that he accepts all believers just as they are. Ask him to forgive you for judging the worthiness of others.

5

Law or Faith?

Read Galatians 3:1–14

Paul had been speaking to the Galatians about Christ's life in the believer. He reminded them that the law had not saved them or made their hearts right before God. The Galatians had accepted the work of the Lord Jesus Christ into their lives by grace through faith, to be saved from the wrath of God. The problem, however, was that after accepting salvation by faith, they then tried to live their new Christian lives by human effort.

Paul reminded the Galatians of how foolish they were for falling into this trap of the false teachers. "Who has bewitched you?" he asked (verse 1). The false prophets had charmed them and deceived them with flattery and flowery wicked arguments. Paul challenged the Galatians to remember that the meaning of the crucifixion of Christ was clearly presented to them. Paul's original preaching to them had plainly told them that Christ's sacrificial death provides full payment for believers' sins. Nothing else is necessary for salvation. It should have been obvious to them that those who preach a salvation through law deny the need of the death of Christ. How could the Galatians be so foolish as to fall for a doctrine that denied the sufficiency of the cross of Christ alone?

Paul then spoke to them about their experience of the ministry of God's Spirit. In the last chapter, Paul reminded them that the difference between believers and unbelievers is the presence of the Spirit of Christ. How had they received the Holy Spirit? Had they received the Holy Spirit by observing the law of God or had he been given to them as a gift of God when they believed the gospel they heard (verse 2)? Does God give his Holy Spirit only to those who measure up to his perfect standard? The Galatians knew that this was not the case. Some of them were of Gentile origin. They had not grown up with the law of Moses nor had they lived godly lives, and yet they knew the presence of God's Spirit in their lives. Had they been required to meet a perfect standard before receiving the Holy Spirit, then none of them would ever have received him.

Paul reminded the Galatians that the Holy Spirit was given to them at the beginning of their salvation (verse 3). Undeserving as they were, they had received this wonderful gift from God (Romans 8:9; 1 Corinthians 12:13). They had begun with the Spirit but had then tried to attain the goal of perfection by human effort.

Have you ever given someone a gift because you knew they needed it only to find that after receiving it, they put it on a shelf and never used it? This is how the Galatians were treating the Holy Spirit. They had never learned to allow him to minister through them. They had never learned how to listen to him. They knew nothing of his empowering and enabling in their lives. Instead, they placed him up on a shelf to admire and went on with life as normal, serving in their own strength and wisdom. What an insult this was to God. God gave his Holy Spirit to us because we need his guidance and empowering. We dare not turn our backs on him and seek to grow and serve in our own strength.

"Have you suffered so much for nothing?" asked Paul in

verse 4. Why would the Galatians suffer the scorn and insults of the unbelieving world when they were living just like them (Acts 14:21–22)? If believers suffer because of the life of Christ in them, that is one thing. It is quite another to suffer because of faulty human strength and wisdom. Had God given the Galatians the benefit of the indwelling Holy Spirit simply to have them set him aside? Was God working miracles among them because they kept the law (verse 5)?

In verses 6–14 Paul attempted to show the Galatians the theological and Biblical basis for what he was telling them. He brought them back to Abraham. He reminded them that in Genesis 15:6 God said that Abraham's belief alone was credited to him as righteousness. In other words, Abraham was considered to be in a right relationship with God not because his conduct was perfect but because of his trust in God alone. To this man of faith, God promised that all nations would one day be blessed (even those who knew nothing about the law of Moses). People from every tribe and nation would be brought into the family of God not because they observed the law and merited the favor of God but because they, like Abraham, believed the gospel when it was preached to them. Those who have faith in God's words are blessed along with Abraham (verse 9). We become the children of Abraham by following his example of faith.

What Paul was showing these Jews was that even their revered spiritual father Abraham was considered righteous not because of his actions but because of his belief in God. It was faith and not works that brought Abraham into fellowship with his Creator.

Having pointed them to Abraham, Paul turned to a second passage of Scripture. Here he reminded them of what Moses wrote in Deuteronomy 27:26. In that passage Moses taught his people that the person who did not continue to do everything that was written in the law was cursed. How many of us have never fallen short of the law of God? To say that we have never disobeyed the law of God would be to say that we were perfect. Every one of us has fallen short of God's requirement. We are all under the curse of the law. The law placed us before an impossible standard. Those who sought to live by the law were condemning themselves to be cursed by God for their disobedience. There was no hope under the law. Why would the Galatians again place themselves under such an impossible standard? If they chose to be judged by the law, they would be condemned. "Clearly no one is justified before God by the law" (verse 11).

Having said this, Paul reminded the Galatians of the plan of God for salvation apart from the law. "The righteous will live by faith," he told them, quoting Habakkuk 2:4. He reminded them of how the Lord Jesus came to rescue people from the curse of the law. He took the curse of the law on himself and offered people a salvation apart from their own efforts (verse 13). By his death on the cross, he provided a legal means of forgiveness for sin and a release from its curse of divine wrath. Through Christ's death even the Gentiles could by faith receive the Holy Spirit, enter a relationship with God, and become part of a spiritual family that had its roots in Abraham (verse 14).

Paul reminded the Galatians that it was God's intention that they live by faith, not by human effort. The law could offer no hope. Their only hope was in the work of Christ on their behalf. Their spiritual life must be lived by faith in what the Lord Jesus had done for them. They were fully forgiven and accepted in him. Nothing they could do would make them more accepted. Their Christian life should have been a loving response to such a wonderful and gracious work because God had already fully accepted them through the work of his Son.

For Consideration:

• Have you ever felt that you needed to serve more, believe more, or have more faith to be more acceptable to God? What does this passage have to say about this?

- Why has God given you his Holy Spirit? To what extent do you depend on the Holy Spirit in your ministry and service?

- Have you ever sensed the Holy Spirit leading you? How did you know the difference between the ministry of the Holy Spirit and your own human effort and wisdom?

- What is the difference between serving God in an attempt to be more accepted by him and serving him from an attitude of full acceptance?

For Prayer:

- Ask God to forgive you for the times you were not sensitive to the leading and empowering of the Holy Spirit.

- Ask God to forgive you for the times you failed to understand that you were completely accepted in Christ whether you served him faithfully or not. Ask the Father to give you great confidence in his Son and his finished work.

- Thank God that he accepts you fully. Ask him to enable you to serve him out of love and devotion, rather than from a desire to be more acceptable.

6

The Purpose of
the Law

Read Galatians 3:15–29

Paul had been telling the Galatians that they were not only saved by faith but also they needed to live by that same faith as well. He had reminded them that they could never be saved by the law. This, of course, caused a real problem for the Jew who misunderstood the purpose of the law and thought that salvation came by keeping the law and by being a physical descendant of Abraham. If it was God's intent to save people apart from the law, why had he given the law to Moses? Paul addressed this issue in this next section of his letter.

The apostle began with the covenant God gave to Abraham and his descendants. This covenant was central to the Jewish religion. The Jews saw themselves as part of a special family. They were the people of God whom he had set apart from the other nations for his own purposes since the time of Abraham. The covenant that God made with Abraham promised that all the nations would be blessed through him. This was God's promise to send the world a Savior. This covenant was based on

God's gracious promise and not on the obedience of Abraham to any law.

In verse 16 Paul reminded the Galatians, however, that the promise God made through Abraham was not to his "seeds," meaning many people, but to Abraham's "seed," meaning one person in particular. In saying this, Paul told the Galatians that this covenant was to find its fulfillment not so much in all the physical descendants that God would give Abraham but in one particular individual (one particular seed of Abraham). That person was the Lord Jesus himself. God's purpose was not just to make Abraham's descendants a great nation but through them to give the world a great Savior. What God would do through the Lord Jesus would be the ultimate fulfillment of the covenant made with Abraham.

In verse 17 Paul stated that God entered into another covenant with the descendants of Abraham several hundred years after the original promise was given to Abraham. The new covenant made through Moses did not replace the Abrahamic covenant. The covenant of law was simply a temporary addition to the covenant of promise until Christ came. The inheritance of blessings promised to Abraham depended on God's grace alone and not on human obedience to any law (verse 18).

If God knew from the very beginning that Abraham's descendants would not be able to keep the law, why did God give it to them through Moses? Paul told the Galatians in verse 19 that the purpose of the law with all its regulations was "because of transgressions until the Seed to whom the promise referred had come." In other words, the law of Moses revealed to the Israelites their need of God's mercy. It showed them how much they needed a Savior. It prepared the way for the solution to the problem of sin. It showed the children of Abraham that God was a gracious God willing to forgive and extend his hand of grace. It also showed them, however, the justice of God in dealing with sin. Without the law no one would have understood the holiness, justice, love, and grace of God. The law shows people who they really are. It also shows them their need of

Christ as the only possible bridge between a sinful people and a holy and just God.

The law, according to verse 19, was put into effect through angels. We do not usually think of angels being part of the giving of the law. But in Deuteronomy 33:2 Moses tells us: "The Lord came from Sinai and dawned over them from Seir; he shone forth from Mount Paran. He came with myriads of holy ones from the south, from his mountain slopes." According to Moses, myriads of holy ones (angels) were present on Mount Sinai when the law was given.

As Stephen defended himself before the Jewish ruling council, he said: "You who have received the law that was put into effect through angels but have not obeyed it" (Acts 7:53). There is a clear sense in these verses that angels were involved in the giving of the law. This adds to the majesty of the law. The law was so important to the purposes of God that he put his angels in charge of preserving it throughout the generations. Satan knew the power of the law to point God's people to their need of a Messiah. We can be assured that Satan has done his utmost to distort people's understanding of it.

The sense of verse 20 seems to be that the covenant of law was mediated between two parties: God and the Israelites. Each party had responsibilities in this covenant. Paul stated in verse 21 that the Mosaic covenant of law did not oppose or replace the Abrahamic covenant of promise. God gave them both for different purposes. The law revealed the need for a Savior, because no one could keep the law as God required. It prepared the way for Abraham's Seed (Christ) to fulfill the Abrahamic covenant. Righteousness would come by grace through faith and the covenant of promise, not through the covenant of law.

Verses 22–24 explain that law, instead of giving life, literally shows that everyone is a prisoner of sin. People are helpless before its perfect standards. It reveals that sinners are separated from a holy God and unable to please him through self-effort. Its restrictions weigh people down under an impossible load. Ultimately the law was designed to show God's people their deep need of salvation by the grace and mercy of a holy God. Paul described the law as a jailer over condemned prisoners, leading them to Christ who would justify them by faith, saving them from the wrath they deserved.

Paul made it quite clear in verse 25 that faith in Jesus Christ removed sinners from being under the "supervision of the law." When Christ came, he perfectly kept the law and presented himself as Israel's true master and guide for holy living. Life by faith in Christ replaced life under the law.

From this point, in verse 26, Paul made it very clear that the promises made to Abraham would ultimately be accomplished through Jesus Christ. Believers are sons and daughters of God, said Paul, not through the practice of the law but by faith in Jesus Christ and his work.

We have all failed in our attempt to meet the standard of God we see in the law of Moses. We are all guilty before God. Those who accept the work of Christ, however, are clothed with Christ (verse 27). What does it mean to be clothed with Christ? Paul explained that believers are baptized into Christ's death, resurrection, and righteousness.

Imagine, if you will, the water in which believers are baptized. As we are immersed in this water, we are covered completely by it. This is a picture of what the Lord Jesus does for us. He comes to wash us clean and immerse us in his righteousness. When God the Father looks on us who are clothed with Christ's purity, he sees the person of his Son and not our shortcomings and failures. He no longer sees the sin and rebellion. All those failures have been forgiven by the death of Christ. No matter what we have done, we can experience the resurrection life of Christ. Spiritual baptism into Christ is promised not only to the Jew but also to the Gentile. Both slaves and free and male and female can know the covering presence of the Lord Jesus by faith. With the presence of God's own Son clothing and filling us, we are "all one in Christ Jesus," united in equality of relationship with God the Father (verse 28).

You do not have to be a physical descendant of Abraham to

be a child of God. You do not have to be able to perfectly obey the law of Moses. If you want to be a child of God, you need to be clothed with Christ. You need his covering presence over your life. You need to belong to him (verse 29). All those who belong to Christ are considered Abraham's descendants and heirs of the promised spiritual blessings God spoke to Abraham concerning his Seed, who is Christ.

What could not happen under the law, Jesus did by his work on the cross. His work is sufficient to forgive all our failures and sin. He is willing to cover us with his presence and righteousness.

Has Christ clothed you with his presence? Have you come to understand that you cannot, by your own effort (by the law), ever please God the Father? Open up your heart by faith. Surrender to him. By faith, let Christ clothe you with his righteous presence.

For Consideration:

• What did Paul say was the purpose of the law of Moses? Can you live in your own strength according to the standard that God laid out in the Mosaic covenant?

• Have you experienced being clothed with Christ? What changes have come about because of this?

• Have you surrendered your entire life to the Lord Jesus, or have you been fighting to do things your own way? In which area of your life today do you seek the Lord's power?

For Prayer:

• Thank God that he graciously forgave your sins through the death of the Lord Jesus?

• Do you know someone who has been trying to merit God's favor by living a good life? Ask God to reveal to this person the futility of this lifestyle.

- Ask God to help you to understand that you no longer belong to yourself but to Christ. Ask him to forgive you for living selfishly and to guide you in righteousness.

7

Sons and Slaves

Read Galatians 4:1–11

What is the difference between the heir to a great fortune who has not yet come into this fortune and a poor slave? While the heir potentially will have a great fortune when it is handed over by the present owner, the slave has no inheritance to look forward to. In many ways, however, the heir's current position is no better than that of the slave. The potential wealth is of no current value because there is no access to it.

In New Testament times, a young male heir was subject to a guardian just as a slave was subject to a master. Even if a young man was the heir to a great fortune, until he reached the age of inheritance, his guardian controlled his life. He could not use his wealth until his father determined that he was old enough and mature enough to handle the responsibility.

Paul used this point to illustrate an important lesson to the Galatians (verses 1–5). All of them had been slaves to the law. Paul said that the law had imprisoned them (3:22–23). Under the law they had been constantly striving to please God but never able to do so. In the end, they were no closer to God. In verses 4 and 5, Paul referred to Christ's divine nature and human nature and briefly stated the doctrine of justification by faith. The Lord Jesus came to rescue God's people from this bondage. In the Father's time, he set his people free from the law by sending his Son to die for them. By his death on the cross, Jesus graciously provided forgiveness and restored relationship with God the Father through faith. This, according to Paul, was the way to escape the control of the guardian law and enter into the wealth of being sons and daughters of God.

God sent the Spirit of his Son into the hearts of believers. According to verse 6, the presence of the Holy Spirit in our lives gives us the assurance of a right relationship with God our Father. The Spirit that God placed in us cries out, "Abba, Father." There is a deep intimacy and assurance in these words. This is not the cry of someone who is unsure of a relationship with God. This is the confident cry of a child for a loving and tender daddy. The presence of the Holy Spirit in our lives places us in the family of God and gives us the assurance of a relationship with him.

Not only this, but the Spirit also releases the resources of God into our lives. Because we are no longer slaves but sons and daughters, we are heirs to all that God has in store for Christ (Romans 8:17). The Holy Spirit places at our disposal all the empowerment and wealth of God. When he comes to live in our hearts, he brings his gifts with him. He comes to release to us our inheritance in Christ.

Do we realize what we have in Christ now that God has sealed a relationship with us by means of the Holy Spirit in our hearts? Through the ministry of his Holy Spirit, God's power and enabling are at our disposal. We have the authority of sons and daughters of the Creator of the universe. We are no longer slaves. How many of us ever tap into the resources that are available to us? How often have we lived like slaves when we have the riches of our Heavenly Father at our disposal? Why should we let sin defeat us when we are more than conquerors in Christ (Romans 8:37)? How can we be defeated when the all-powerful Spirit of Christ lives in us?

In verses 8–11 Paul rebuked the Galatians because they were not living as mature children of God but as slaves. Prior to coming to know Christ, their lives consisted of a slavery to rules and regulations. The difference between a slave and a son not only has to do with wealth but also with relationship. A slave relates to a master simply on the level of rules and generally does not have a close relationship with the master. On the other hand, a son enjoys a very different relationship and can cry out, "Abba, Father." A son benefits from an intimacy and an honored position that a slave could never have.

What kind of relationship do you have with God? So many people are content to live as slaves according to the law when they could have a deeply intimate relationship with their heavenly Father. Their faith does not mature in love and devotion to God.

Paul wrote, "You are observing special days and months and seasons and years! I fear for you, that somehow I have wasted my efforts on you" (verses 10–11). The Galatians did not understand what they had in the Lord Jesus. They were content to be slaves when they could live as privileged sons and daughters. They were content with dead rules when they could have had a living relationship with their Creator. Look back in verse 9 to see what Paul thought about the reduction of faith to rules and regulations. He called laws "weak and miserable principles."

We cannot take this lightly. These are strong words. There is nothing wrong with the observation of special days and months. Very often we observe these practices as a way to honor the Lord. The problem, however, is that we need to move beyond these principles. A faith that does not grow beyond observing certain practices is a very shallow faith indeed.

As a son, I have potential for a wonderful relationship with my heavenly Father. This ought to be my focus. Rules will never satisfy the longings of my heart. What the world around me needs is not more rules but a relationship with my loving Father. In a close relationship there is joy, peace, satisfaction, and fulfillment. Observing rules, however good they are, will not save or satisfy the deepest needs in our souls. Only a personal relationship with God can do this.

Paul challenged the Galatians to reconsider where they were in their relationship with the Lord Jesus. They were living as young children who had never claimed their inheritance. They were not enjoying the richness of their spiritual blessings made possible by faith in Christ. They were not rejoicing in a close relationship with the Lord God through the Spirit. They were content with spiritual immaturity, but Paul was calling them to the spiritual freedom of their inheritance in Christ. This passage gives us cause to reflect on our own relationship with God.

For Consideration:

- What is the difference between a son or daughter and a slave? How have you been living? Explain.

- What are the privileges of spiritual inheritance? Are you presently enjoying these privileges?

- What is the place of rules and special observances in the Christian life? When do they become a hindrance to our relationship with God?

For Prayer:

- Ask God to help you to understand what it means to live as his son or daughter.

- Thank him that while he does expect you to live in obedience to him, your relationship with him is much deeper than what you do for him.

- Thank the Lord for the depth of relationship he wants to have with you. Ask him to forgive you for not entering into that relationship as you should.

- Ask the Lord to help you to tap into the resources that are at your disposal in Christ. Thank him for his ample provision of all that you need.

8

Hagar and Sarah

Read Galatians 4:12–31

I n 2 Corinthians 3:14–16 Paul wrote: "But their minds were made dull, for to this day the same veil remains when the old covenant is read. It has not been removed, because only in Christ is it taken away. Even to this day when Moses is read, a veil covers their hearts. But whenever anyone turns to the Lord, the veil is taken away." Paul was saying that there is a veil that covers all who place themselves under that law of Moses. This veil produces darkness and heaviness. It is quite easy to spot those who are living under the law. They are constantly striving but never arriving. The law seems to take away their joy and rest. Only in Christ and his accomplished work can anyone know rest and peace with God.

As Paul began this section of his letter, he reminded the Galatians of his first encounter with them. According to verse 13, it was because of an illness that Paul first preached the gospel to the Galatians. We know nothing of the details of this sickness. During that time Paul became like one of them (verse 12). The Galatians had accepted him as one of their own. He had become dearly loved like a member of their own family. Paul's sickness seemed to endear him to the Galatians. In verse 14 he reminded them of how they had accepted him as an angel of God. They showed no contempt for him and his illness. Paul knew that they would have torn out their own eyes and given them to him if it would have helped him (verse 15).

While he was with them, Paul shared the message of freedom from the law by the death of Christ. The veil was stripped from their eyes. The Galatians experienced freedom and the joy of the Lord. As Paul looked back on his time with the Galatians, he remembered happy times. Despite his sickness Paul was blessed by God. The Galatians happily accepted Paul's gospel preaching. They opened their hearts to the gospel and were set free to experience the joy of the Lord through freedom from the law.

As time passed, however, false teachers came to Galatia and turned the hearts of the Galatians back to the law. What was the result? In verse 15 Paul asked: "What has happened to all your joy?" It seems that the Galatians, by returning to the law, had lost their joy in the Lord and even turned against Paul (verse 16). They had turned from the truth Paul preached and placed themselves under the veil again. They had gone back to using the Mosaic law as their guide for life instead of being guided by the Spirit. They had gone back to trying to merit God's favor by their good deeds instead of trusting in the finished work of Christ.

Paul warned the Galatians about these false teachers who were very zealous but wrong. They wanted to separate the Galatians from the clear teaching of the apostles and gain a following for themselves (verse 17). Paul encouraged the Galatians to be zealous for the truth that he had taught them and not depart from it in his absence (verse 18).

Paul saw the Galatians as his dear spiritual children (verse 19). He had brought them to Christ. He had done so through tremendous pain and difficulty. We have already seen that he came to them in sickness. Beyond this, however, Paul suffered much for preaching the gospel. He compared this suffering to the labor pains of a woman giving birth. As his suffering endeared him to the Galatians, it also endeared the Galatians to Paul. They were his children, and he had endured many trials to see them mature in their faith. Paul was very upset as he saw their freedom in Christ being destroyed by false teachers. In verse 20 Paul told the Galatians that he wished he could be with them in order to guide them back to the truth.

To illustrate to the Galatians the contrast between being under law and being under grace, Paul used an Old Testament story and compared the son of Hagar (Genesis 16:1–16) with the son of Sarah (Genesis 21:1–7). He reminded the Galatians of how Abraham had two sons, Ishmael and Isaac, and the Galatians were in danger of aligning themselves with the wrong son. Ishmael's mother was a slave named Hagar, and he was born by natural means, illustrating reliance on human effort. Whereas, Isaac's mother, Sarah, was free. Isaac was born by supernatural means, illustrating reliance on God. Isaac was born as a result of a promise and miracle of God to a barren and elderly woman. Isaac was a special son of grace (verses 22–23).

Paul used Hagar and Sarah to represent two different covenants: law and grace (verse 24). Hagar represents Mount Sinai where Moses received the law of God. Hagar, the slave, represents all those who are under the law (verse 25; 3:23). She represents earthly Jerusalem with all its imprisoning customs and traditions. Sarah, on the other hand, represents the Jerusalem that is heavenly and free. She also represents all those who are free from the bondage of the law through the grace of the Lord Jesus. It was through Sarah and her child that the promises of God were fulfilled. Abraham's inheritance would fall not on the son of the slave woman but on the son of promise.

Paul quoted a passage from Isaiah 54:1 where Isaiah reminded his people that the blessing of the barren woman would be greater than those of the woman with a husband (verse 27). Paul reminded the Galatians that they were Sarah's offspring, children of the promise (verse 28). The life of Christ in them was not the result of natural human effort; it was a supernatural gift from God. As Isaac's life was a supernatural gift to Sarah, so Christ's life was a supernatural gift to the Galatians.

As Ishmael was born through the sinful union of Abraham and Hagar, Ishmael represents the life of human effort. It is the life of striving to please God by natural means. Isaac was very different because he was born in a supernatural way. His was a miracle birth given to a woman who could not conceive children. He represents the life of Christ planted in us from above as a gift of God. This is what the Lord Jesus does for us. He comes to place his life in us in a very supernatural way. Like Sarah, we cannot produce that life by natural means or human effort. It is a gift from God given to us by faith.

Even as Ishmael mocked and persecuted Isaac, so it will be for all who are born again by God's Spirit (verse 29). Paul experienced this persecution himself as he taught this doctrine of salvation through Christ apart from the law. Paul reminded the Galatians that the Word of God is clear that Ishmael, the son of the slave woman, would not share the inheritance of Isaac, the son of the free woman. It is very important that we understand what is being said here. Those who live under that law will not receive their inheritance in Christ. If you want to inherit the blessing of the father, you need to be born as a child of that father. Paul is telling us that only those who are born again by means of the miraculous work of the Spirit of God can inherit the blessings of their heavenly father. No slave will inherit a son's blessings.

Paul was confident that those to whom he wrote were no longer sons of slavery (verse 31). Paul was stating here that there are two types of births. When humans are born by natural means, they are born enslaved to sin and death. By natural human effort, no one can please the Lord and merit his salvation. But those who are born again by spiritual means are freed from sin and death. By God's grace and through faith, God's own life is planted in the souls of believers as his Holy Spirit comes to live in them. God sees his own life in them and recognizes them as his children. Let us praise the Lord who saved us out of slavery to the law of sin and death and planted his own life in us.

For Consideration:

- How do those who place themselves under the law sacrifice the joy and peace of the Lord in their lives?

- Is it possible to be a child of promise, like Isaac, and live like Ishmael, the son of a slave? What are the characteristics of a person living under the law?

- How can the miraculous birth of Isaac be compared to what happens to people who receive the Lord Jesus into their lives?

- Why will those who have not been supernaturally born of God not inherit eternal life?

For Prayer:

- Ask God to help you to live as a child of the promise and no longer to trust in your own natural efforts to please him or merit his grace.

- Thank God that he accepted you as one of his own children by grace and rescued you from bondage to sin and death.

- Thank the Lord for the joy that comes from your full acceptance before God through Christ's work without any effort of your own.

- Do you know some people who do not understand their need of spiritual birth? Ask God to reveal himself to them.

9

The Preaching of Circumcision

Read Galatians 5:1–15

In chapter 4 Paul told the Galatians that they were children of Sarah, the free woman, and they needed to live in the freedom that was theirs. They needed to claim their inheritance as sons and daughters of God and live in the freedom of their full acceptance in Christ apart from the law. In the first verse of chapter 5, Paul reminded the Galatians that they had been set free by the Lord Jesus from the law. It was not his will that they be bound any longer to the Mosaic law. Their freedom had cost Christ his life. How could they go back to bondage when they had been freed from it at such a high cost?

Paul made a strong point in verse 1: "Stand firm, then," he said, "and do not let yourselves be burdened again by a yoke of slavery." Paul also used the expression "stand firm" in Ephesians 6:14 when he spoke about spiritual warfare. The idea of standing firm can be illustrated by a soldier who digs in and refuses to surrender his ground to the enemy. Paul felt very strongly about falling back under the law. For Paul, slavery to the law had no place in the life of the true believer. He challenged the Galatians to resist the false teaching among them with all their might.

Paul focused in this section on the act of circumcision. When Paul spoke of circumcision, he spoke about the sign of the Abrahamic covenant (Genesis 17:9–14). God required that every male Israelite child be circumcised. This was a sign that they belonged to God. Anyone who did not have this sign in his flesh was to be cut off from the people of God. No uncircumcised male could belong to God.

Under Christ all this changed. According to Paul in verse 2, if a person let himself be circumcised in order to earn salvation, he was saying that the death of Christ was to no avail. If parents believed that by circumcising a son they were guaranteeing him a place in the family of God, they were diminishing the work of Christ.

If circumcision or any other human effort could make a person righteous, then why would Christ have had to die? The sacrifice of Christ cannot benefit anyone who trusts in ritual acts of self-effort for salvation. In verse 3 Paul reminded the Galatians that if they wanted to earn salvation by keeping the law, they had to keep the whole law perfectly. But if they couldn't perfectly observe the whole law of Moses, then they gained nothing by observing only one command. Returning to the covenant of law was, in reality, saying that they didn't need Christ and his salvation by grace.

Paul was saying that it is either all one way or all the other. Either people can be saved through the law or they can be saved through the work of Christ. There is a clear choice to be made. Both roads cannot be taken at the same time. People must follow one or the other. Paul reminded the Galatians, however, that the road of law would ultimately lead them to failure and condemnation and away from the saving grace of Christ (verse 4).

The alternative to "trying to be justified by the law," according to Paul, was to wait by faith for the final righteousness that comes from Christ (verse 5). What did Paul mean?

Righteousness means being innocent, not guilty, before God. Paul was telling the Galatians that whereas the law of Moses could never give them this innocence, believers in Christ receive it as a gift. There is also the hope of a future, perfected righteousness that comes when believers are glorified in heaven (Romans 8:18–25).

Paul went on to say: "Neither circumcision nor uncircumcision has any value" (verse 6). Circumcision has nothing to do with salvation. The only thing that matters is "faith expressing itself through love." What is this faith that Paul spoke about here? The object of faith is the work of the Lord Jesus. Instead of vainly trusting in their own efforts to achieve righteousness, Paul wanted the Galatians to trust in the righteousness that comes by faith in Christ.

Some people might say that this type of faith would encourage the believer to sit back and do nothing. If we are trusting in what the Lord Jesus has done for us, then why should we worry about loving God or others? Notice that Paul tells us that saving faith expresses itself through love. That is an important statement. When faith is genuine, it is active and loving. Saving faith will love the Lord Jesus for what he has done and love others, following the example of Christ. Paul wanted the Galatians to serve God out of love, not out of a sense of trying to merit acceptance by human effort.

The Galatians had begun on this road of faith expressed though love. They had experienced God's gracious acceptance of them despite their sin and rebellion against him. They were running a good race, but someone cut in on them and distracted them into running the wrong race (verse 7). Paul reminded them that the people who were cutting in on them were not from God (verse 8). Those who taught acceptance by God through the law were enemies of God. Like yeast in a lump of dough, they would quickly infect the whole church. One by one, people were being deceived and falling away from the truth of faith expressed through love.

According to verse 10, the teachers who were leading the

Galatians into error would pay a very serious penalty for their evil deeds. This was not just a different opinion on a minor point of doctrine. The false teachers were, in fact, diminishing the importance of the cross of Christ. They were instruments in the hands of Satan to turn eyes from the gracious person and work of Christ. They were guilty and would certainly have to pay the price for their evil.

Paul showed the intensity of his feelings toward these false teachers when he said in verse 12: "I wish they would go the whole way and emasculate themselves." Paul had righteous anger against these preachers of heresy because they were pre-senting false doctrines that diminished the work of the Lord Jesus on the cross. They were agitating the flock of God and causing confusion and disunity in the church. They could not be tolerated because they were poison to the body of Christ. And God would judge them harshly.

Lest the Galatians misinterpret what Paul was saying, he reminded them in the closing verses of this section that while they were called to be free, that freedom did not give them the right to "indulge the sinful nature" (verse 13). He chal-lenged them to serve each other and to love their neighbor as themselves (verse 14). This moral requirement of love from the Mosaic law (Leviticus 19:18) had not changed with the coming of Christ. The Galatians needed to be careful to lovingly serve one another so that the opposing factions did not destroy the church.

Being set free from the law through the forgiveness of Christ gives us an entirely new motivation for serving God. We serve him because we are thankful for his acceptance and forgiveness of us by grace apart from obedience to a code of rituals. We serve him out of gratitude for what he has done.

Through the Spirit, Jesus enables us to serve him with a whole new power. I can now delight in serving from faith working through love. It is no longer my obligation to serve him through external rituals specified by a strict code of law; it is my joy and delight to serve through the Spirit. I still live to please God, but now I act from a motivation and power that comes from the Holy Spirit.

For Consideration:

- Why is it such a serious matter to teach that people can get to heaven by their works? How does this depreciate the work of the Lord Jesus?

- What is the difference between serving to be accepted and serving from a stance of full acceptance?

- If we are fully accepted by God, does this mean that we can live as we please? Explain.

- Do you serve the Lord out of obligation or out of joy and delight?

For Prayer:

- If your service to the Lord is characterized by obligation, ask the Lord to set you free from the spirit of religion and law. Ask him to restore to you the joy and delight of service through the Spirit of love.

- Thank God for what the Lord Jesus accomplished on the cross for you. Thank him that in Christ you are fully accepted.

- Ask him for wisdom to stand firm against the subtle attacks of the enemy to have you turn from the grace in Christ.

10

Living by the Spirit

Read Galatians 5:16–26

Paul made it amply clear that we have been set free from the law by the death of the Lord Jesus. That freedom, however, does not give us the right to indulge the sinful nature. It gives us, on the contrary, a new way of serving the Lord. We now serve from a heart that delights to do the will of God. What brings this change? It is the presence of the Holy Spirit in our lives. The Holy Spirit sets the believer's heart on fire with passion for the Lord Jesus, his work, and his Word. In this section Paul encourages the believer to live by the Spirit.

Paul began in verse 16 by telling the Galatians that they were to live by the Spirit so that they did not gratify the desires of the sinful nature. In saying this, Paul was telling them that they had a choice to make. They could continue to live according to the desires of their flesh, or they could live according to the Spirit. Paul encouraged them to live by the Spirit. Paul listed for the Galatians in verses 19–21 some of the acts of the sinful nature. He seemed to classify these acts into four major types. Let's examine them briefly.

Sexual Perversions

The sinful nature expresses itself in sexual immorality, impurity, and debauchery. The enemy excels in perverting sexuality. While the sexual appetites are normal and proper in their context, the sinful nature does not restrain itself within proper boundaries. Its desire is to satisfy the appetites of the flesh. It cares nothing about the ways of God. It should be understood here that sexual immorality is not limited to physical acts but includes mental acts as well. Jesus taught in Matthew 5:28 that people can be guilty of sexual immorality in the mind as well as in the flesh. Impure thoughts are included here in Paul's description of the acts of the flesh. In our day as never before, the sexual appetite is being encouraged through the entertainment industry by means of pornography in its various forms. How much damage has sexual immorality caused to the families of our nations? How many homes have been broken because of the temptations of this fleshly foe?

Spiritual Perversions

The acts of the sinful nature can also be spiritual in nature. This spirituality, however, is perverted. Idolatry and witchcraft are the fruits of this type of perverted spirituality. Idolatry has to do with the worship of anything other than the one true God. These idols vary from place to place. Sometimes they are made of wood or stone. In other cultures these idols come in the form of luxurious houses and big bank accounts. The names of these idols may vary, but they all draw attention away from the one true God.

Witchcraft has to do with the manipulation of the spirit world for personal gain. Witchcraft enters into communication with the powers of darkness. This may include such things as reading horoscopes or palm reading done in a seemingly innocent manner. The spirits behind these practices are demonic. Psychics may make predictions, but they do not derive their power from God. Their destructive and seductive power comes from the devil.

Broken Relationships

Another aspect to the sinful flesh is that it produces broken relationships. Hatred, discord, jealousy, fits of rage, selfish ambition, dissension, factions, and envy are all the natural fruit of the flesh. The flesh does not consider the needs of others. It is selfish in nature. It will fight to get what it wants even if that involves harming another person. The flesh is out to please itself at all costs. It resents anything that stands in its way. The devastation caused by this can be seen in the wars that ravage our world. Our prisons are filled to overflowing with those who surrendered at one point or another to the sinful flesh and lashed out in anger and jealousy at their fellow human beings.

Breakdown of Society

A final aspect to the acts of the sinful flesh has to do with the results in society. The sinful flesh loves company. Paul reminded the Galatians that evidence of the flesh can be seen in the drunkenness and partying that goes on in a society. In verse 21 Paul showed the Galatians how the sinful flesh was at work in the core of their society. There were those who lived to drink, party, and satisfy the lusts of the flesh. They banded together with others of like mind and encouraged each other in their sinful desires and lusts. This drunken partying spirit can still be found at all levels of society, from the rich and famous to the poor and downcast. Paul told the Galatians that this spirit was not of God, and those who habitually live like this are not believers (verse 21).

Paul encouraged the Galatians not to get caught up in these things. He encouraged them to live by the Spirit in order to overcome these fleshly desires. In verse 17 the apostle had reminded them of how strong the pull of the flesh really is, even causing them to do those things they did not even want to do.

We have all experienced this in many different ways. Very often we do not plan to fall into sexual immorality or angry outbursts—but it happens. How often have we spoken angry words that we never intended to speak? Not too many of us actually plan to fall into sin. We have a very powerful foe in our flesh. How is it possible for us to have victory over such a foe? Paul had already told the Galatians that the only way was to live by the Spirit (verse 16).

What does it mean to live by the Spirit? We know what it means to live according to the sinful desires of the flesh, that is, to surrender to their power in our lives. If we are to live by the Spirit, it will mean surrendering to his influence in our lives instead of the influence of the flesh. This will mean putting aside our own selfish ideas and attitudes. It will mean trusting less in what we can do and waiting for the Spirit of God to work through us. Those who live by the Spirit submit to the Spirit's control of their lives. To do this we need to know how to listen for his leading and obey his promptings. When God saved us from our sin, he placed his Spirit within us to conform us into the image of Christ. Through reading the Scriptures, prayer, and depending on the Holy Spirit, we can cooperate with God in accomplishing in us what he has promised to do (see Philippians 1:6; 2:13).

What will be the result of letting the Spirit of God take control of our lives? He will produce in us his own fruit. The fruit of the Spirit is contrary to all the fruit of the flesh. We need to examine briefly here the fruit of the Spirit.

The Spirit of God will produce in us the fruit of love (verse 22). This love is a selflessness that reaches out to others even when it knows it will get nothing in return. The Spirit will also produce joy and peace. These are the result of being in a right relationship with God. We were created for God and will never know true joy and peace until we are in a right relationship with him. Outside of him there will only be restlessness and emptiness. God's Spirit also fills us with patience. Patience is the ability to remain faithful despite the opposition that comes our way. This patience will work itself out in relationships with people around us. The Holy Spirit gives us a confidence in God that enables us to wait on him.

Kindness, goodness, faithfulness, and gentleness will also be produced in our lives. We will be concerned for others with sincere consideration. We will be seeking their good. We will be trustworthy in our relationships with those around us. While the flesh seeks immediate gratification, the Spirit produces self-control in the life of the believer. The believer is not controlled by his moods or passions.

Paul reminded the Galatians in verse 23 that there is no need for a law for those who are being controlled and led by the Spirit. The natural fruit of the Spirit will produce increasing righteousness in the life of the believer. Spirit-controlled believers do not need the law as an external guide to the Father's will because they have the internal guide of God's own Spirit.

If I belong to Jesus, I have died to my old nature. In surrendering to the Lord Jesus, I offer him my life to use as he sees fit. I keep on turning my back on my old way of thinking and yield to him. As a believer, I keep on choosing to live by the Spirit and welcome the Spirit of God to dwell in my life to use it to bring glory to Christ.

Paul challenged those who had received the Holy Spirit to keep in step with that Spirit. In saying this he was reminding them that it was possible to have the Holy Spirit in them but not be keeping up with him. It is easy for us to lose touch with the Spirit of God and begin to produce the fruit of the flesh by becoming conceited, provoking and envying others (verse 26). There is no neutral ground; either we are actively living in step with the Spirit's leading or we are actively giving in to our sinful desires.

As believers, our greatest desires in life should be to keep in step with the Spirit. Only as we submit to him by grace can we experience his power and enabling. Only as we are in step with the Holy Spirit can we live for and glorify the Lord Jesus. It is vital that we stay in the Word and in prayer in order to be guided by the Spirit of God. The normal Christian life ought to be one of hearing from and yielding to the Spirit of Christ who lives in us.

For Consideration:

- What are the cravings of the sinful nature? Do you see evidence of the flesh in your society? Give some examples.

- What evidence is there of the presence of the Holy Spirit in your life?

- How can we conquer the deeds of the flesh in our lives as believers?

- Are you keeping in step with the Holy Spirit? Are you aware of his working and leading in your life?

For Prayer:

- Thank the Lord that he has given us his Holy Spirit to rule in our lives.

- Ask the Lord to open your heart to the ministry of the Holy Spirit in a deeper way.

- Take a look at the fruit of the Spirit in verse 22. What fruit do you appear to lack? Ask God to produce that fruit in your life.

- Ask God to help you keep in step with the Holy Spirit in your life.

11

Concluding Comments

Read Galatians 6:1–18

P aul had been reminding the Galatians that their freedom from the law should never cause them to indulge the sinful nature. He challenged the believer to "keep in step" with the Spirit of God. While our relationship with the Lord is very personal, it is not in isolation from other believers. Paul reaffirmed in this section the importance of the community of the body of Christ.

Paul challenged those who were spiritual (walking in step with the Spirit) to restore those who were caught in a sin. According to Paul, the restoring of believers caught in sin is an obligation for every spiritual believer. Be assured that Satan will do his utmost to hinder this process. He will fill our minds with all kinds of excuses why we should not speak to our brothers and sisters about their sin. Paul told the Galatians that this was the only loving and compassionate thing to do.

Notice, however, how we are to speak to a brother or sister caught in sin. First, we must be walking in harmony with the Holy Spirit before approaching anyone about sin. In the gospels Jesus reminds us about judging our brother or sister for the speck in their eye when we have a plank in our own (Matthew 7:3). If we are not living for the Lord ourselves, what authority do we have to speak to others about their sin? We can only lead people as far as we ourselves have gone.

Second, notice that the restoration needs to be done gently. It is easy to be judgmental and harsh. We often show far less compassion and mercy for sinners than God does. I have seen believers look down on others for falling into sin. I have seen churches deal harshly and severely with those who have fallen. Remember how the Lord dealt with the woman caught in adultery (John 8). Her fellow human beings wanted to stone her to death, but Jesus showed great mercy and compassion. He dealt with her gently. What sinners need, very often, is a compassionate hand to help them up. We have all seen fallen believers dig themselves deeper into their sin simply because of the response they received from their church. Instead of lovingly helping them back to their feet, fellow believers shunned them and cast them aside. Paul challenged the Galatians to have the attitude of Christ in restoring a brother or sister.

Third, we see in verse 1 that this process of restoration needs to be done in humility. Notice that Paul told the Galatians that they needed to restore their brother or sister with the understanding that if they did not watch themselves, they could easily fall into the same sin. When we speak to others, we need to realize that we too could have fallen. We dare not be so arrogant as to assume that some sins are beyond us. We are all just a single decision away from falling into a similar sin. We all have a sin nature. We should let the understanding of our own fragile spiritual condition influence how we speak to a brother or sister who is snared in sin.

In light of the temptations all around, Paul challenged the Galatians to carry each other's burdens. What did he mean by this? If you want to carry your brother's burden, you need to know what your brother's burden is. I am coming to realize that the body of Christ is full of burdens. There are people coming to our churches each week who are weighed down with heaviness. They often leave the same way. If we are to carry each other's burdens, we must open ourselves up to each other. We must learn to provide opportunities for people to open up to us in a deeper way. We need time with people to understand what they are going through.

Do you have spiritual friends that you can open up to? Are there people in your church with whom you can share your deepest hurts and wounds? Do the people in your church allow you to share these things? A healthy body needs this sort of accountability and love. One of the most important functions of the body of Christ is to minister one to another in this way. To ignore this principle is to seriously weaken the body of Christ.

In this ministry of restoring believers and carrying each other's burden, it is quite easy for us to begin to compare ourselves to others. We can look at the problems a brother or sister is going through and feel superior. When we see others falling into sin, we can puff ourselves up and think that we are more spiritual because we did not fall into the same trap. In verse 4 Paul encouraged the Galatians not to compare themselves to anyone else but instead to judge their own actions. God will not judge us on the basis of whether we lived as good a life as a brother or sister. We are accountable to God for our own personal obligations and ministry callings.

Comparing ourselves to others only leads to pride and jealousy. This is not of God. In verse 5 Paul told the Galatians that each of them was to carry his or her own burden. In other words, we are not to impose our standards on others. Just because you are able to pray for two hours each morning does not mean that you have the right to impose that standard on someone else. You may be responsible to God for those two hours of prayer each morning because the Lord may have called you particularly to that ministry, but your brother may not have that same ministry. You must carry your own God-given responsibility without imposing your spirituality on someone else. God works in us all differently.

Paul changed his focus in verse 6. He encouraged those who were being taught the Word of God to share their finances with those who were teaching them. In those days evangelists and teachers traveled throughout the area. Their only means of support were the gifts and contributions that came from the believers they taught. Paul encouraged the churches to stand behind these true teachers of the Word.

In verses 7–10 Paul stated that people would reap what they sowed. Paul had been telling the believers of Galatia that they needed to let the Spirit of God work in them if they were to live according to the law of Christ. To some people this meant sitting back and doing nothing. Paul challenged this attitude. Surrendering to the Spirit of God is hard work. We reap what we sow. If we continue to believe the lies of the enemy, how can we expect God to fill us with his truth? If we continue to allow bitterness and jealousy to grow in our hearts, will it not grieve the Spirit of God? If we continue to sow and cultivate sin, we can expect to see more and more sin grow in our lives. If, on the other hand, we surrender to the will of God, we will see the fruit of the Spirit taking root in our lives.

Walking in step with the Spirit is hard spiritual work. Daily we need to die to ourselves and our own ideas. Daily we need to take up our cross and crucify our sinful desires. At times we wonder if we will ever have victory over the sinful acts of the flesh. Paul encouraged the Galatians in verse 9 not to become weary in doing good. Persevere in resisting the devil, and he will be forced to flee from you (James 4:7). Keep sowing seeds of righteousness, and you will harvest in due time. What an encouragement this is for us. Not all victories come overnight. Some come after long and hard resistance, but all victories come by the grace of God and not through our efforts alone.

In verse 10 Paul told the Galatians that they were to do good one to another as often as they had opportunity. The battle before them was long and hard. They could not face the enemy alone. They needed each other. They needed support and encouragement. They needed people to share their burdens. The

Christian life is a team effort. Each person needs to play his or her part if we are going to win the battle.

Paul concluded his letter with some final comments in verses 11–18. He pointed out to the Galatians that this particular letter was written by his own hand in large letters. This gives us the impression that the apostle struggled with poor eyesight. Could this have been a result of seeing the glory of God on the road to Damascus? Was this his thorn in the flesh? We are not clearly told.

He warned the Galatians again about those who were teaching circumcision. These false teachers were very impressive with their flowery and flattering words, but their motives were wrong. They wanted to observe the Mosaic law so they would impress others by their external religion. They were afraid of being persecuted for the gracious message of the cross. They did not have the courage to take a stand for the Lord Jesus. They compelled the Galatians to be circumcised merely to glory in numbers of converts (verse 13). The only thing believers should ever boast in, Paul told the Galatians, is the cross of the Lord Jesus because it is their only hope and glory (verse 14).

It does not matter whether a person is circumcised or not, concluded Paul. What is important is whether the person is a new creation in Christ (verse 15). Has the Holy Spirit of Christ come to dwell in our hearts? Have we become new creatures through the inner work of forgiveness and sanctification by the Holy Spirit of Christ? This is what matters. When we stand before the Lord Jesus on that final day, he will not check to see if we have been circumcised. He will not be interested in what church we attended. He will not even be looking for how many good deeds we did while we were on earth. The only thing he will be looking for is whether the Holy Spirit lives in our hearts.

Paul concluded in verse 17 by reminding those who would cause him trouble about the wounds he bore in his body for the proclamation of the truth. He was not ashamed of the gospel. He saw these wounds as a badge of honor. He wore them as a soldier would wear his medals. These wounds were the marks of someone who stood firmly for the truth.

In the opening verses of this book, Paul reminded the Galatians of his calling as an apostle. In the concluding verses, he showed them that he had been faithful to that calling. He bore in his body the marks of a faithful servant. He wished them Christ's necessary grace for their continued relationship with God and with each other.

For Consideration:

- Do you know a brother or sister in Christ who is presently wandering from the truth? What does this section teach us about how to deal with this person?

- Why is it so difficult for believers to open up to each other? How can we bear each other's burdens if we do not share our lives with each other?

- What do we learn here about the importance of humility in restoring each other?

- Paul tells us to carry our own burdens. How easy is it to impose our responsibilities on others? Why is this wrong?

- Why is it dangerous to compare ourselves to others?

For Prayer:

- Ask God to help you to be more open to your need of the body of Christ in your relationship with him.

- Ask God to give you a deeper compassion and mercy for those who have wandered from the path. Take a moment to pray for such a brother or sister.

- Ask God to help you to deal with the ways in which you have been sowing seeds of the flesh in your life.

- Ask God to help you to accept the differences that exist in the body of Christ in our day.

Ephesians

12

In Christ

Read Ephesians 1:1–14

Paul opened his letter to the Ephesians by informing them that he was an apostle of Jesus Christ by the will of God. His apostleship was not a career decision he made himself. It was a ministry to which he had been called by God and that brought with it certain responsibilities and obligations. What Paul wrote to the Ephesians carried the authority of God.

Paul's desire was that the Ephesians experience the grace and the peace of God in their lives. Grace and peace are often associated with salvation, but Paul's desire for the Ephesians was that they continue to experience these blessings in large measure on a daily basis. How easy it is for us to lose a sense of God's favor and its resulting condition of peace. The enemy delights in robbing us of the awareness of these blessings.

In verses 3–14 Paul exploded in one long sentence of praise and worship of the God and Father of our Lord Jesus Christ for all he has done for believers. He has completely blessed us in the heavenly realms, Paul told his readers. The apostle made a distinction here between our earthly blessings and our spiritual blessings in the heavenly realms. On this earth we have received many blessings. Our health and possessions are all from the hand of a loving and compassionate God. These in themselves are tremendous gifts from God. Paul's focus, however, was not on our material blessings but the spiritual blessings we have received. Because we are united with the Lord, our spiritual lives are already in heavenly realms with him. What are these blessings? Let's look at them one at a time.

He Chose Us in Him before the Creation of the World (verse 4)

Before the creation of the world, the Creator of this universe had a plan: he chose us to be holy and blameless before him. It was the desire of the Lord God from the beginning of time that we should belong to him and live in victory over sin. Holy means set apart and blameless means without blemish. Because we were chosen and created with this purpose in mind, we will only understand true happiness and joy in life if we are living in this holiness.

It is the will of God for believers to be victorious over the world system, the flesh, and the devil. We do not have to live defeated lives. The God of this universe has created us for victory. How many times have we given in to our sins, believing that we could never experience victory? Satan has been successful in blinding our eyes to the sins that still remain in our lives. "Don't worry about those little sins," he tells us. How often have we believed his lies and continue to live with our sins? Knowing that I have been created and chosen from the beginning of time to be holy and blameless before God ought to cause me to strive to that end. In a world caught up in evil, what a privilege it is to be specially called and enabled by God to live out the righteousness we have been given in Christ.

In Love He Predestined Us to Be Adopted as His Sons (verse 5)

Not only have we been chosen to be conquerors, God has also chosen us to be his sons and daughters. There is intimacy in this verse. God is interested in much more than us living in victorious purity. He wants a personal relationship with us as well. As sons and daughters of God, we have the privilege of entering into his presence and sharing our hearts with him. As his sons and daughters, we are inheritors of eternal life in his riches. The Father's blessings are poured out on us. He promises to care for us and guide us as his children.

Why should the great God of this universe enter such a relationship with us? He does so "in love." It is love that motivated him to adopt us as his children. Notice that this was in "accordance with his pleasure." In other words, God reached out and adopted us as his children because it was his pleasure to do so. This tells us something about God. It brings him pleasure to relate personally and intimately with his children. So desirous was he for us to enter this intimacy with him that he sent his Son to die on the cross so that, through the forgiveness of our sin, we could know him as our loving heavenly Father.

We have never had anyone else love us like this. What wonderful grace—that God would send his beloved Son to die for us so that we could know him. What a blessing it is to be adopted as children of God and to know how deeply he longs for communion with us. This ought to move our hearts to worship and praise him for his wonderful, free, and sovereign grace toward us. This is the ultimate purpose of our salvation—the glory of God who is gracious toward sinners.

In Him We Have Redemption through His Blood (verse 7)

Paul reminded the Ephesians that, as children of God, they had redemption through the blood of Christ. We were not adopted as God's sons and daughters because we earned his favor. The fact of the matter is that we were far from God. As lost sinners, we were separated from the holy God. We were enslaved to sin and under divine wrath. In love, God sent the Son to buy us out of this slavery. It cost Jesus his life, but he willingly and lovingly paid the price so that we could be freed. God planned this because he is a gracious and compassionate God. Because of this redemption, our sins have been forgiven. We will never suffer God's wrath. Never will we have to pay the great price for our rebellion against God. The Lord Jesus paid it all. Paul reminded the Ephesians of the tremendous burden that the Lord took with him to the cross so that the Father could lavish his gracious forgiveness on his chosen ones.

He Made Known to Us the Mystery of His Will (verse 9)

Notice in verse 8 that God not only redeemed believers by Christ's blood but he also lavished on them wisdom and understanding. God's grace toward believers was not exhausted in redemption. Paul told the Ephesians that God's grace was also abundant in making known to them the mystery of his will. That is to say, he delighted to give them insight into his purpose and plan. What is that plan? Verse 10 tells us that it is a plan to bring all things back under the dominion of Christ. One day everyone and everything will be submissive to the righteous rule of the Lord Jesus.

This is what God is doing in this world. This is the reason why he brought us to himself by redeeming us from our sins. God's full plan will be accomplished in his own time. Verse 11 contains one of the strongest statements in Scripture of the sovereignty of God: he "works out everything in conformity with the purpose of his will."

God revealed to us this plan for Christ through his Holy Spirit and through his Word. We have the privilege of seeing this plan unfold before our eyes and in our lives. We have the opportunity to be part of this wonderful divine purpose. God delights to include us in the outworking of his purposes for this planet. What a blessing this is!

The apostle Paul saw in his day a partial fulfillment of this wonderful plan as men and women were being rescued through his ministry from the jaws of the enemy. Today we are seeing an even greater fulfillment of that purpose in the world as God's Spirit moves in power conquering the power of the devil. In verses 12 and 13 Paul reminded the Ephesians that the Jews were the first to be chosen by God to hope in Christ, and through the Jews God's purposes were being worked out in Gentile lives as well. God brought the Ephesians to himself so that they, in turn, would bring praise to his holy name. What an awesome privilege it is not only to be given the understanding of this great work of God but also to be part of its outworking.

You Were Included in Christ When You Believed (verse 13)

On the day we believed, we were brought into the family of God. We were placed in the body of Christ. As children of God, we have been marked with a special seal—the Holy Spirit of God. The presence of the Holy Spirit in our lives is a guarantee not only that we belong to the Lord Jesus but also that nothing will ever be able to separate us from the Lord Jesus and our spiritual inheritance.

The Holy Spirit is compared in verse 14 to a deposit that guarantees our inheritance. The presence of the Holy Spirit in our lives is a stamp of God's approval. The Holy Spirit comes to live in our lives and to empower us in the work that God calls us to do. He comes to produce in us the character of the Lord Jesus. He will continue this work in us, Paul said, until the day of our final redemption. Until that time God has placed his Holy Spirit in us to enable us to live for him. He is a foretaste of the glory that is to come.

In this opening section of the book of Ephesians, Paul described for the Ephesians some of the wonderful blessings that were theirs in the Lord Jesus Christ. They had been chosen by God before the world began to live above the sin and evil of this present age. They had been adopted as God's sons and daughters. Christ had bought them for God at the cost of his blood. God had made them part of his wonderful plan to bring all things under the headship of Christ. He placed his Holy Spirit in them as a seal of his approval. How we need to praise the Father for these wonderful blessings that he has graciously given to all believers in Christ.

For Consideration:

* Are there any particular sins that you cannot seem to overcome in your life? What does this section of Scripture teach you about God's desire for you to live victoriously?

- What evidence is there in your life of the hand of God on you even before you came to know the Lord Jesus personally?

- What does this section teach about God's desire for intimacy with you? Do you experience this intimacy with God? What keeps you from knowing it more deeply?

For Prayer:

- Thank God for the blessings Paul spoke about in this section.

- Ask God to help you to live as his child. Ask him to forgive you for the times you chose to return to the things of this world.

- Thank him for his Holy Spirit who lives in you. Ask God to help you to be more sensitive to the leading and work of the Holy Spirit.

- Thank the Lord that he did not give up on you but pursued you until you came to him.

- Ask the Lord to help you to live a life of holiness. Ask him to give you victory over any recurring sin.

13

Growing in Him

Read Ephesians 1:15–23

Oune of my favorite hymns is "My Jesus I Love Thee." One line in this hymn reads, "If ever I loved thee, my Jesus 'tis now." Every time I sing this hymn, I find myself asking, Do I really love Jesus more now than I ever have? Do I love him more today than yesterday? Have I actually grown in my relationship with him? These are very important questions we all need to ask ourselves. All too many of us are happy simply to remain baby Christians. Becoming a Christian is just the beginning. Paul's desire for the Ephesians was that they move forward in their relationship with the Lord. He wanted to see them grow into maturity. As much as we love our little children, none of us would want them to remain children all their lives.

In the last section, Paul told the Ephesians of their position in Christ. They had been chosen and sealed by the Holy Spirit of God. God delighted to include them in his wonderful plan to bring all things under Christ. Having informed the Ephesians of their blessings, Paul then prayed for these saints. Paul praised the Lord in verse 15 that the Ephesians had been brought into this wonderful relationship with the Lord Jesus. He rejoiced when he heard about their faith in the Lord Jesus and their love for the saints. Paul did not want them to stop at that point, however. God had even greater plans for the Ephesians, and Paul wanted them to reach their full potential in Christ.

Notice in verse 16 that Paul did not stop giving thanks for what God had already done in the lives of the Ephesians. But he also continued to ask God for a deeper work of his Spirit in their lives. Over the next few verses, Paul shared with the Ephesians his prayer for them.

That God Would Give Them the Spirit of Wisdom and Revelation (verse 17)

Paul began by asking God to give to the Ephesians "a spirit" (NKJV) of wisdom and revelation so that they would know Christ better. What is this spirit of wisdom and revelation? Paul was not speaking about human insight. He was crying out to God that the spiritual eyes of the Ephesians would be opened to see Christ in a new way. He was praying that God would reveal himself to the Ephesians, not in intellectual truths learned in books but through deep and intimate experience. The goal of this wisdom and understanding was not information but knowing Christ in a deeper way.

Do you have this spirit of wisdom and revelation? Is your heart burdened to know God? Do you cry out for more revelation of his character? Do you hunger and thirst for his presence? Paul's cry for the Ephesians was that they would not be happy with where they were in their spiritual walk but that they would be constantly crying out for more and more of Christ.

That the Eyes of Their Heart Would Be Enlightened (verses 18–23)

Paul also prayed that the eyes of their heart would be opened to see three vital truths. The first truth that Paul prayed the Ephesians would see was the hope to which they had been called (verse 18). What was this hope? Paul had already given part of the answer to this question in the first section of this chapter where he spoke to the Ephesians about their spiritual blessings in Christ. He reminded them that they were chosen to be blameless before God (verse 4). As believers, they were called to live in victory over sin. They were chosen to be children of God and inheritors of his great kingdom. They were also partakers in the unfolding of God's great purpose of bringing the whole world under the authority of the Lord Jesus. They were sealed with the promise of the Holy Spirit of God who is a guarantee of things to come. As believers, they had a tremendous hope. They had been called and enabled to live in victory. The knowledge of this victory ought to have stirred them to new heights. Paul wanted the Ephesians to live in the marvelous hope that God had called them to.

Paul also wanted the Ephesians to grow in their knowledge of the riches of their glorious inheritance in the saints (verse 18). The riches that Paul spoke about here are the riches that we have "in the saints." In the first section of this chapter, Paul spoke about our spiritual blessings in Christ in heavenly realms. Here, however, Paul wanted the Ephesians to know the riches that God had given them in each other. How often we fail to understand the tremendous blessings we have in each other. God has called us to live in community. He has created this community in such a way that it will not function properly unless each member contributes a part. All the gifts in this body of believers work together for the advancement of the kingdom of God. Satan trembles when he sees the body of Christ working together in harmony. Could it be that this is the reason why he spends so much time trying to divide and sow seeds of disorder into the church?

Have you ever sat back and thought about the wonder of your own body? Have you ever been amazed at how the eye can see and the ear can hear? Have you ever found yourself standing in awe at the complexity of the human brain? This physical body is a wonder to behold. I remember standing beside my wife when each of our children was born, tears streaming down my cheeks at the wonder of life itself. The spiritual body of Christ is no less marvelous. In recent months I have been astonished to see how the body of Christ can work in such harmony. I have seen the hosts of hell flee as the body of Christ rose up in one mind and exercised their spiritual gifts for the good of the whole. Paul prayed that the Ephesians would come to a deeper understanding of what they had in each other.

Third, Paul wanted the Ephesians to grow in their understanding and experience of the power of the Lord Jesus in their lives. God has placed his Holy Spirit in us. He has given us authority in his name to conquer. He has chosen to use us as the instruments of his power in this world. How little of this we understand. Paul reminded the Ephesians that the power that God had put at their disposal was the same power that raised Christ from the dead (verse 20).

It is a power far above any power, title, or authority, not only in this age but also in the age to come. This is a power that can send the forces of hell into retreat. It is the power that conquered nature and the grave. It is the power of him who fills everything in every way. It is the power of God, and this universe in all its vastness cannot contain it. This power can be seen in the force that makes the smallest cell live. It is also demonstrated in the beauty of the universe. There is no place this power cannot be seen. There is no place it cannot be felt.

While this power is not for us to do with as we please, it is, nonetheless, at our disposal. What God authorizes he also grants power and authority to do. Do we understand the power that is at our disposal? How often have we hid in our little corners not knowing what to do while the enemy ravaged our homes and churches?

Paul's desire for the Ephesians was that they would come to a deeper understanding of their authority and power in Christ and that they would take their stand against the forces of the enemy in Christ's name without fear or shame. He wanted the Ephesians to grow in their relationship with the Lord. He prayed that God would give them hearts that longed for him in deeper ways. He prayed that God would give them a deeper awareness of their hope in Christ, the riches they had in each other, and the power of God that was at their disposal. May God grant to us a deeper awareness of these same vital truths.

For Consideration:

- Have you been content with where you are in your relationship with the Lord Jesus? What challenge did Paul bring the Ephesians here?

- What evidence is there of spiritual growth in your life?

- What blessings do you enjoy from being part of a family of believers?

- What evidence is there of the power of God in your life? What power does God put at your disposal? How have you tapped into that power?

For Prayer:

- Ask God to give you a greater desire to know him.

- Ask God to give you a deeper awareness of the power that is available to you through the work of the Lord Jesus and the ministry of his Holy Spirit in your life.

- Thank God for the Christian family he has given you. Ask God to help that family grow in ministry to one another.

14

Alive in Christ

Read Ephesians 2:1–10

P aul's prayer for the Ephesians was that they grow in their understanding of the work that the Lord Jesus had accomplished in their lives through his death on the cross. Here in this section the apostle continued to remind the Ephesians of what took place in their lives when they came to the Lord Jesus as their Savior. We need to examine what Paul taught the Ephesians here about their relationship with the Lord.

You Were Dead in Your Transgressions and Sins (verses 1–2)
Paul began by reminding the Ephesian believers of their spiritual condition before they came to Christ. "You were dead in your transgressions and sins," Paul told them. The deadness to which Paul made reference here is spiritual death, which is the absence of communion with God. The unbeliever is described as dead, not just sick or weak in purity and truth but dead to it. Notice the result of this spiritual death in their lives.
Verse 2 tells us that before salvation, the Ephesians had

lived in their transgressions ("false steps") and sins ("missing the mark"). They lives were dominated by rebellion against God. Notice also in verse 2 that they once followed the world's way of thinking. If the world told them that they needed a bigger house, they would have believed it. If the world told them that they were unimportant unless they had lots of money, they would have believed this also. They were controlled by the world's way of thinking and did not understand the ways of the Lord.

You Were Controlled by the Ruler of the Kingdom of the Air (verses 2–3)

Before coming to the Lord Jesus, the Ephesians were dominated by the ruler of the kingdom of the air—Satan himself. Paul reminded the Ephesians that Satan is at work in those who are disobedient to God's ways. Satan had once used the flesh and the world to keep the Ephesians away from the Lord Jesus and his salvation. Satan had once kept the Ephesians trapped in evil systems and wicked thoughts. He had blinded them to the greater realities in Christ. They had been snared in the petty desires and fleshly cravings of the sin nature as Satan kept bombarding them with worldly ideals and false philosophies. In 2 Corinthians 10:4–5 Paul referred to these philosophies as fortresses in which unsaved people are imprisoned.

As human beings, we have been created in the image of God with a capacity to enjoy and commune with God. This is what distinguishes us from the animals, which are not spiritual beings. The problem, however, is that a spiritually dead person is content to live like the animal kingdom, gratifying only physical and emotional needs.

You Were Objects of God's Wrath (verse 3)

Paul told the Ephesians that when they were dead to God and lived in the way of the world, the flesh, and the devil, they had been under the condemnation of God. God's divine wrath is very real and righteously directed toward all ungodliness and rebellion. Sin keeps the disobedient far from God. They do not realize that they are on a path that leads to eternal condemnation because Satan and the world blind them to truth. This does not change the fact that all unsaved people are on a road that leads straight to hell.

It is very sobering to realize that, like the Ephesians, once we all were "by nature objects of wrath." All unsaved people are in this dangerous condition. Some have never heard that the path they are on is leading them to eternal separation from God. Others do not believe this truth although they have heard it. But people's unbelief does not nullify God's truth, which Paul was stating here. The enemy blinds those who are separated from God, and they do not even know that they are under God's eternal condemnation.

God Made Us Alive in Christ (verses 4–5)

Paul, speaking for all believers, stated that our merciful God lovingly rescued us out of our dangerous predicament. He saw us spiritually dead, blinded, and held captive by the enemy, our own sinful natures, and the ways of the world. In love God took us from the jaws of Satan, death, and hell. Through the gracious forgiveness of our sins by the work of Christ, God gave us life when we were dead. He planted his own life in our dead souls, giving us spiritual life. God did all this for us by grace and not because we deserved it.

Things radically changed for us when we became alive with God's own life. In reality, we became brand new people (see 2 Corinthians 5:17). God's Holy Spirit gave us a new appetite for the Word of God and the things of God. We experienced a new passion for holiness. The Spirit of God began to take control and produce spiritual fruit in us (see Galatians 5:22–26). We began to receive truth and were empowered to behave in a new way.

God Raised Us with Him and Seated Us in Heavenly Places (verses 6–7)

Next, Paul told the Ephesian believers that not only did they experience new life but they were also lifted up to heavenly places. What did Paul mean by this? First, he was saying that they were now citizens of heaven (see Philippians 3:20). Through the forgiveness of their sins, they had been given a new citizenship. They were now sons and daughters of God. As children of God, they could look forward to their heavenly inheritance. This world was no longer their home, and they lived as foreigners on earth. They were spiritually raised up with Christ and seated in heavenly places where he is.

For all believers this is not merely something we look forward to at a future date. We experience even now the reality of these heavenly realms. Our desires and attitudes are being changed from worldly to spiritual. We know first hand communion with the Father. His joy, peace, and love are our present experience. We have been set free from the corrupt mentality of this present world. We have a higher standard and a higher calling. We have been lifted up from the deadness of this world and its philosophies to spiritual union with Christ in heaven.

Through all these blessings, God is demonstrating the richness of his grace and mercy (verse 7). It is important that we realize that the Lord God is pleased to glorify himself through us. By filling us with his power and love, he brings honor and praise to himself now and in the eternal ages to come. By showering us with his peace and joy, he shows the world that he is a loving and compassionate God. He delights to reveal his character through individuals like you and me. What an honor it is to be a channel of this blessing to others. It is beyond our imagination that the great and holy God of this universe would want to use us to be a channel of his mercy and grace to others.

This Salvation Is All of God's Grace (verses 8–9)

How can we experience this new life? What do we have to do to participate in this wonderful blessing of becoming alive in Christ? Verses 8 and 9 remind us that it is simply by God's grace that all this is possible. There is nothing that anyone can do to merit this new life and blessing. God gives his life to spiritually dead sinners by grace (unmerited favor). No one can be good enough, or live well enough, or do anything special enough to gain salvation. God grants this new life simply on the basis of his good pleasure. All we can do is receive what he gives us.

This is a humbling thought for many of us. We would like to think that we were saved from our sins because we deserved it somehow (see Romans 3:10–20). We would like to think that God saw some good in us and said, "I need to save those people because I can see how hard they are trying." This is not what the Bible teaches. The more we try to merit the favor of God, the farther we fall from the truth of what grace is. It is a free gift given without consideration of merit and solely based on God's sovereign choice. This is what the Lord does for us. He offers to us free of charge and with no prior qualifications this wonderful salvation as an absolutely free gift, simply because he wants to give it to us for his own pleasure.

We Were Created for Good Works (verse 10)

Paul reminded the Ephesians that they were created in Christ Jesus to do good works. God saves his chosen ones from the world in order that they might be his servants in this world to bring glory to his name. Believers are rescued from the world in order that they might return to the world with the life of Christ. They are saved so that God's grace and kindness are demonstrated through them to a world blinded by the enemy. They are his instruments for good works so that people might see those good works and bring glory and honor to our Father in heaven (Matthew 5:16).

While our salvation is absolutely free, it will cost us our lives. We who are saved are required to live for God in return. We are to be his instruments in this world and the next for the glory of his name.

For Consideration:

• What influence has the world's way of thinking had on you? How does this differ from God's way?

- Have you experienced this new life of Christ? What evidence is there of his life in you today?

- Paul tells us here that we have been lifted up into heavenly realms in Christ. How are you living in heavenly realms today?

- Why is it so hard for people to accept this salvation as a free gift? Why is it so hard to accept something we have never worked to merit?

- What is the difference between working to merit our salvation and serving out of gratitude to God for his full acceptance of us?

For Prayer:

- If you have never experienced this new life in Christ, take a moment to ask the Lord to reveal his life in you.

- If you know the life of Christ in you, ask him to reveal himself in an even greater way through you. Offer your life to him afresh as an instrument of his blessing to others.

- Take a moment to thank the Lord for some very specific changes he has made in your life.

- Ask the Lord to enable you to be an example of good works for those around you.

15

No Longer Strangers

Read Ephesians 2:11–22

The Lord Jesus has done many wonderful things for us. Paul was trying to communicate to the Ephesians the incredible riches they had in the Lord Jesus Christ. In this section he reminded them of yet another wonderful reality that came with their new relationship with the Lord Jesus.

Under the Old Testament system, the Ephesian Gentiles were strangers to God. They were known as the "uncircumcised." As such, they were excluded from the elite family of God and from his covenant purposes for his people. Gentiles were without God and without hope in this world. As strangers to the covenant of God, they were bound to an eternal separation from God and under his divine wrath. There was nothing they could do about this. What a tragedy this was. Eternal separation, eternal wrath, eternal agony awaited them in the world to come. I do not think that any one of us has a real understanding of what this really means. This too was our destiny apart from God's grace. As foreigners to the covenant of God, we were excluded from citizenship in his kingdom.

With the coming of the Lord Jesus to this earth and his death on the cross of Calvary, Gentiles, who were once strangers to God and his covenant purpose, could become part of his kingdom. Christ's death broke down the social, spiritual, and covenantal wall that separated Jews from Gentiles (verse 14). The blood of Christ satisfied the wrath of God against the sins of both Jews and Gentiles. The life and death of the Lord Jesus abolished the Old Testament's Mosaic covenant that uniquely separated Jews from Gentiles.

The work of the Lord Jesus on the cross of Calvary instituted a new covenant through which God would deal with humans. In the new structure, every believer in Christ is on an equal footing. Spiritually speaking, a believer in Christ is no longer a Jew or Gentile, but a Christian. No longer does a person have to be born a Jew to be part of the divine promises. No longer does a person have to bear the sign of circumcision to be accepted by God. No longer does a person have to offer the blood of bulls and goats at the temple to symbolize the forgiveness of sins. No longer is God's covenant comprised of a strict set of rules and regulations. The Lord Jesus, by his death, provided a means whereby anyone, regardless of religious or cultural background, could come to him directly and be forgiven of their sins. His death abolished the ancient covenantal divisions.

According to Paul, the Lord Jesus died so that both Jews and Gentiles could become one (verses 15–16). Christ came and preached peace to the Gentiles who were far away from God. He also preached this same message to those Jews who were the chosen children of God. In Christ there is no longer a division between Jews and Gentiles. All of us can know peace with God and a hope of eternity in his presence. Through Christ's death we now have access to God (verse 18). Gentiles, who were at one time strangers to the covenant of God, now have equal access, rights, and privileges with Jews to stand before God by faith in Christ.

The body of Christ is like a spiritual building comprised

of believers from all walks of life and every nationality (verse 19). It is comprised of people with various denominational distinctions. The Lord Jesus himself is the cornerstone of this great building of his people (verse 20; 1 Peter 2:5–6). The prophets and the apostles built a foundation on Christ and his work. Gradually this great building rose up from its early beginnings. It has become in our day an impressive structure. In it are believers who are Baptists, Pentecostals, Presbyterians, and others. Both the rich and the poor have a place in this great building. The African, the Indian, and the Canadian all add their different flavors. God is adding daily more and more human stones to his wonderful building.

This building, Paul told the Ephesians, was becoming the dwelling place of God Almighty (verse 21). He dwells with his people by his Holy Spirit. Our enemy Satan has been trying to destroy the work God is doing. This universal church strikes fear into the heart of Satan. It represents everything that Satan has been fighting against. Through this body of believers, God is rescuing people from the jaws of Satan and his kingdom of darkness. God is empowering his people to tread on the serpent and to extend the kingdom of his light. Through this church God is building up a people who will bring glory and honor to his holy name.

It should not surprise us that Satan should focus so much of his attention on trying to divide us and blind us to the reality of the power of God at our disposal. Paul told the Ephesians that this body that Christ is building is comprised of both Jews and Gentiles. If they were to mature as God intended and to pierce the kingdom of darkness with the light of the gospel of Christ, they would have to realize that they could not be fighting each other. The Lord Jesus came, Paul told the Ephesians, to bring peace between Gentiles and Jews in order that his presence might be revealed through them to the world.

While believers may not be divided any more on the Jew-Gentile issue, the church of Jesus Christ today is certainly divided over many other issues such as church government and practices. Often we become critical and judgmental of each other. These attitudes only hinder the work of God and remove his full blessing from our midst. How we need to remember that God is building us up as a dwelling place for his Spirit. May we not be a hindrance to this by wrong attitudes and prejudices.

For Consideration:

- What does Paul tell us here about our condition without the Lord Jesus and his work?

- Take a moment to consider the composition of your own local church. What tribes, nationalities, and races attend your church?

- What sorts of divisions exist in the body of Christ in our day? What is the challenge of this passage to us?

For Prayer:

- Thank God for the way in which he is bringing together people from different walks of life and different perspectives to be a dwelling place for his Holy Spirit.

- Ask God to forgive you for your wrong attitudes and prejudices toward other members of the body of Christ.

- Ask God to break down the dividing walls that have been built between true believers today.

16

Paul, Apostle to the Gentiles

Read Ephesians 3:1–13

In the last meditation, the apostle Paul reminded the Ephesians that they were part of a new body of Christ that consisted of both Jews and Gentiles. Through his death on the cross, the Lord Jesus broke down the barrier that existed between these two groups. To ensure that the Gentiles entered this new relationship, the Lord Jesus called the apostle Paul to a ministry of making known the salvation that was freely offered to them.

Paul reminded the Ephesians that he was a prisoner for the sake of the Gentiles. The ministry to which the Lord had called him was not an easy ministry. In order to proclaim the truth of salvation to the Gentiles, Paul had to suffer much (2 Corinthians 11:24–28). On his missionary journeys, he was beaten and stoned. Often he was insulted and cursed by the people he sought to win. Beyond this was the reaction of the Jewish community to his preaching to the Gentiles. As he wrote this letter, the apostle was in prison because of his preaching to the Gentile community. Although he was being held by Roman authorities, Paul considered himself a prisoner of the Lord Jesus (verse 1). He knew that every detail of his life was ultimately controlled by his Lord.

Paul had been called by God to a very particular vision and focus in administering God's grace to the world at this particular time in history (verse 2). He came to this understanding by means of a direct revelation from God (verse 3). The word "mystery" in verses 3 and 4 refers to a truth that was hidden in Old Testament times but was revealed in New Testament times to God's people through the apostles and prophets. Paul explained this mystery to the Ephesians in verse 6: In one new body of believers, the Gentiles would be co-heirs together with the Jews in the promise of eternal life through faith in Christ alone. In one unified church, there would be no racial, social, or spiritual distinctions. This message burned deeply in the heart of the apostle Paul, and he was suffering greatly in order to proclaim it. It was his desire not only to see the Gentiles come to a knowledge of the Lord Jesus but also for them to be fully and equally integrated into the larger body of Christ with the Jewish believers. Paul often took up the defense of the Gentiles against those who believed that they needed to follow the Mosaic law to be saved.

While there are prophetic passages in the Old Testament that allude to the fact that the Gentiles would also become the children of God, this was never clearly understood by the Jews (see Genesis 12:3; Isaiah 49:6). Many Jews believed that Gentiles would have to be first converted to the Jewish faith in order to enter into the blessings of the promises of God. It did not enter their minds that the Gentiles could become fellow heirs together with them without the practice of the law of Moses. The full realization of these prophetic passages did not come until the Lord Jesus had risen from the dead. It was the apostles who began to experience the leading of the Lord to go to the Gentiles. The first major reference to this was when Peter had a vision to go to see Cornelius (Acts 10). In this vision the Lord told Peter that the Gentiles were heirs together with the Jews in Christ apart from the law. Peter had already seen the Holy Spirit come equally on the Gentiles and the Jews at Pentecost (Acts 2:11, 38–39).

While Peter had a vision of God related to the salvation of the Gentiles, it would be Paul who would carry this message to the far corners of the earth. Paul would be the instrument of God to see that the church of his day accepted these Gentiles as equal members of the body of Christ. Paul mentioned in verse 3 that the Lord Jesus had made this wonderful truth real to him by means of a revelation. We are not exactly sure when he received this revelation from God, but it is certain that this revelation was life transforming for the apostle. Remember that Paul was a Pharisee, a very strict observer of the law of Moses. Prior to his conversion, Paul would have held all the beliefs of the Jews of his day regarding the unworthiness of the Gentile community for salvation. Nothing short of a direct revelation of God would have changed his mind about this point. While we are not told how this revelation came to Paul, we do know that he was so convinced of the equal place of the Gentiles in the body of Christ that he willingly risked his life to spread this message.

Paul knew that he was unworthy to be a servant of Jesus Christ (see verse 8). He had for many years persecuted the church. Despite his terrible background, the Lord Jesus did call him to this ministry. Along with the calling came a divine gifting through the "working of his power" (verse 7).

How important it is that we experience, like Paul, both the calling and the gifting through the power of Christ. For many years I knew the calling of God on my life to be his servant, but I was exercising my calling in human strength and wisdom. I was diligent in prayer and study. I was faithful through the difficult times and persevered in what I believed God had called me to do. The problem, however, was that I was doing it all in my own strength. My messages were carefully prepared and worded but lacked the power of God to change lives. I shared the gospel but saw no conversions to Christ. I knew my calling but, for the most part, had turned my back on the spiritual gifting of God necessary to perform that calling. I needed to get out of the way so that the power of God could be demonstrated through me. I had gone through Bible school, university, and seminary and knew biblical truths.

Paul was also a very well-educated man. His education, however, was not what God needed. God gave to Paul a gift through the "working of his (God's) power" (verse 7). This gifting was not through his education or experience. He did not become effective because he went to a conference and learned how to do the work of ministry. The power he received was through the working of God's power in his life. The calling was wonderful, but it was not enough. He needed also to be empowered to perform that calling. This is what I was missing for so many years on the mission field. I praise God that even though I was depending on my own strength, God was able to use my efforts for his glory. But how much more effective I could have been had I been trusting in God's power and not in my own human strength and education.

Paul saw it as his ministry to reveal the mystery of the church to everyone (verse 9). God was unfolding his ancient plan, which had been previously hidden from the world. What a privilege it was, however, for the new believers in Christ to realize that God was unfolding this plan before their eyes. It was the plan of God that through the church his redemptive purpose would be revealed to rulers and authorities in the heavenly realms (verse 10).

Who are these rulers and authorities in the heavenly realms? There are several possibilities. First, the rulers of the heavenly realms may refer to the angelic beings or those who have gone on before us who are now in heaven. The problem with this, however, is the fact that the angels are not generally seen as rulers or authorities in heaven. They are seen rather as servants. God alone is the ruler and authority of heaven.

Another possibility is that these rulers of the heavenly realms refer to Satan and his angels. In Ephesians 2:2 Satan is described as the ruler of the kingdom of the air. Could it be that Paul was saying that God is using the church of Jesus Christ to proclaim his victory to the hosts of Satan? Through this church God is making his glory and honor known to the prince of this world (Satan). The church is the battleground where God and Satan are waging war. God is revealing his glorious victory over Satan and his angels by building this church to his glory.

Satan is doing his best to keep the church in the dark, but the Spirit of God is spreading the light of the gospel by means of the church of Jesus Christ. God's eternal purposes are being accomplished through the church. Men and women of all backgrounds are being rescued from the darkness of this world and coming to realize that through faith in the Lord Jesus alone, they can approach God with freedom and confidence. That simple truth has been devastating the kingdom of darkness.

Gentiles who had been held in the darkness of their sins were coming to realize that in Christ there is freedom and victory. For such a long time, Satan had been successful in holding whole nations captive. The apostle Paul had been chosen to proclaim liberty to these nations. The kingdom of God was moving forward to penetrate the darkest corners of the globe. The church of Jesus Christ was going to be unleashed on the kingdom of darkness. We are still seeing the conquest of Satan's territory in our day.

Paul reminded the Ephesians that this penetration of the kingdom of light into the darkness would not be without its casualties. Paul himself had suffered much. The enemy would not be quick to release his territory. Paul told the Ephesians not to be discouraged because of his sufferings (verse 13). God uses all righteous suffering to spread his glory to believers.

We ought to expect to suffer for the gospel. We ought to be rejoicing at the way the kingdom of God is expanding throughout the world and bringing the light of Christ wherever it goes. May God strengthen us to endure persecution for the spread of victory over evil through faith in Christ alone.

For Consideration:

- Paul had a very clear vision of what God wanted from him. What is God's vision for you? Are you, like Paul, willing to suffer for the advancement of that vision?

- What encouragement do you receive from the fact that God forgave and used Paul who had persecuted the church?

- What evidence is there in your community of the extension of the kingdom of light into the kingdom of darkness?

- Are you serving Christ through your own strength or by means of the working of his power in you? How can you tell the difference?

For Prayer:

- Thank God that he is expanding his kingdom into the darkness of this world. Thank him that he uses us in this great task.

- Ask God to give you a clear vision of your role in the expansion of his kingdom.

- Thank God that he is willing to forgive our sins and use us as his servants.

- Ask God to break down any walls that stand between believers today.

17

Paul's Prayer for the Ephesians

Read Ephesians 3:14–21

Paul's deep concern for the Ephesians is very evident in this letter. That concern led the apostle very often to pray for them. We have already seen some of Paul's requests for the Ephesians (1:15–23). Here again he reminded them of his prayer for them. He told that they were part of a large family in Christ in which there is no difference between the Jew and the Gentile. There is only one heavenly Father. All who are born into his family through the blood of the Lord Jesus are equal brothers and sisters. Paul was part of that family with them. As their brother in Christ, he prayed for them. Let's examine Paul's prayer for the Ephesian believers.

That God Would Strengthen You with Power (verse 16)
Paul's first request for the Ephesians was that they would be strengthened with power through God's Spirit in their inner being. No matter how far they had advanced in their Christian walk, they needed to be strengthened even more. How often have we become satisfied in our walk with the Lord and not

grown? Paul challenged this attitude. Paul prayed that the Ephesians would never stop growing in their relationship with the Lord Jesus. It was his desire that they be strengthened more and more in faith.

Notice here that Paul desired that they would be strengthened with power. What was the source of this power? It came from the glorious riches of God through his Spirit who lived in them. The power that Paul spoke about here was not a physical power but a power in the "inner being." This is the place where the Spirit of God comes to live in every believer. Paul was praying that the Holy Spirit of God would be revealed more and more in the inner being of the Ephesians. This could only take place as they learned to yield to his ministry. Paul was not speaking here about greater human effort. He was speaking rather about a deeper work of the Holy Spirit of God in the lives of the Ephesians, enabling and empowering them to grow in faith.

That Christ May Dwell in Your Hearts through Faith (verse 17)

The whole purpose of being empowered by the Holy Spirit of God was so that the Lord Jesus might dwell in their hearts by faith. How are we to understand this verse? Doesn't the Lord Jesus live in every believer's heart? While the Lord Jesus is in the heart of every believer, not every believer welcomes that presence in the same way. There are some believers who, because of their love for the things of the world, resist the fullness of Christ's life in them. Paul's prayer was that the Father would strengthen these believers through a mighty work of the Holy Spirit so that the presence of Christ would dwell more powerfully in them. The ministry of the Holy Spirit is to exalt the Lord Jesus through intimate fellowship with believers.

That They May Be Rooted and Established in Love (verse 17)

The result of Christ dwelling in his fullness in their hearts would be that they would be rooted and established in the fullness of God's love. How important it is to feel secure and loved in our relationship with the Lord. Without that security we fall prey to temptation. The enemy will attack us at this level and seek to cause us to believe that God doesn't care about our situation. He will lead us to believe that God has abandoned us in our problem or that God will not be there for us when we need him. It is God's desire that we be rooted and established in the love of his Son for our spiritual protection.

As a husband, I know how important it is for me that my wife be sure of my love for her. I want her to know that no matter what happens or no matter how hard things may get between us on any given day, my love for her will never change. It is God's desire that we be secure in our relationship with his Son. He promises us that nothing can separate us from his love (Romans 8:39). He tells us that he will never leave us or forsake us (Hebrews 13:5). He reminds us of his willingness to forgive us for all our offenses (1 John 1:9). It was the prayer of Paul for the Ephesians that they would know that the love of the Lord Jesus for them would never change. Knowing this would give them courage to seek forgiveness and boldness to face the foe. It was his prayer that this love motivate them to new heights of obedience and service.

That They May Grasp the Love of Christ (verses 18–19)

Paul also prayed that the Ephesians would not only understand the security of their position in Christ but that they would also be able to grasp the immensity of Christ's love. In verse 19 Paul told them that this love surpassed knowledge. In other words, they would never be able to thoroughly grasp the love of Christ for them, but he wanted them to grow in a fuller experience of it. He wanted them to always stand in awe of this marvelous love of Christ who gave himself for them. Those who know Christ best, marvel the most at his love. There should always be a sense of awe and wonder in our hearts when we think of the vastness of his love for sinners. Each day we should be coming to a deeper appreciation of his love for us.

That You May Be Filled with the Fullness of God (verse 19)

Paul wanted to see the Ephesians filled with the full presence of God in their lives. He wanted to see them dying to themselves and experiencing the power, love, and majesty of God in their thoughts and actions. When people looked at them, they would see God shining through them. Paul wanted the Ephesians to experience the fullest measure of God through total devotion to him.

As we think about what the apostle Paul was saying here, we are left wondering if we could ever experience this sort of life. Is it really possible to experience the glory of God in our lives? Paul concluded this section by reminding the Ephesians that God was able to do far more than they could ever ask or imagine (verse 20). The power of his Holy Spirit within them could accomplish divine and miraculous things beyond their vision.

We can experience everything that the apostle spoke about here. Notice, however, that we will never be able to accomplish this in our own strength. This sort of relationship with God can only be accomplished by the powerful working of the Holy Spirit within us.

Don't resist what God wants to do through his Holy Spirit in your life. Learn to surrender to his leading and prompting by staying in the Word and in prayer and in fellowship with other believers. Trust the Father to lead you deeper and deeper in the love of Christ. Only then will you begin to experience the reality Paul was speaking about here.

Just the simple thought of what God wanted to do in the lives of the Ephesians brought Paul to a place of worship. He concluded this section of his letter with praise: "To him be glory . . . throughout all generations, for ever and ever!"

For Consideration:

- What is it that keeps you from experiencing the fullness of God's love for you today? What things get in the way?

- Are you being strengthened with power in your inner being? Is there evidence of the presence of the Lord Jesus in your life today? In what ways has he been revealing his power in you?

- What do we learn here about our secure position in the Lord Jesus?

- What does this passage teach us about God's desire for us as believers? Where do you fall short personally?

For Prayer:

- Thank God for the fact that his love for you is certain. Can you think of specific times when the security of his love was an encouragement to you? Thank him specifically for these times.

- Ask him to open up your heart to the ministry of his Holy Spirit in your inner being. Ask him to forgive you for the times you have resisted his working in your life.

- Ask him to show you areas of your life that have not yet been willingly surrendered to the Lord Jesus. Ask him for grace to surrender these areas to him.

18

Living Lives Worthy of Our Calling

Read Ephesians 4:1–6

In the first three chapters of this letter, Paul had explained to the Ephesians their position in the Lord Jesus Christ. They had been rescued from the jaws of the enemy and adopted into the family of God. There were certain obligations that went with being a child of God. Here in this section, the apostle challenged the Ephesians to live lives that were worthy of the calling that they had received. He spoke to them as a prisoner of the Lord Jesus who understood the consequences of living a pure and bold life. Paul expected nothing less of the Ephesians. Even as their Lord had been willing to die for them, so they too needed to be willing to lay down their lives for him.

Notice that Paul reminded the Ephesians that they had each received a calling from God (verse 1). What was that calling? It was the calling to be children of God. Being a Christian is not only a privilege of position but also a calling to holy living. Each of us who has come to the Lord Jesus and experienced the wealth of his life has been called to live for him. Seeing my relationship with the Lord Jesus as a calling should stir up within me a sense of obligation and duty. I have been saved from the world to be a servant of the Lord Jesus in this world. Paul began to explain to the Ephesians that a worthy life requires the control of the Holy Spirit. This idea sets the theme for the last three chapters of this book.

Be Humble (verse 2)

"Be completely humble," said Paul to the Ephesians. This attitude of humility is best seen in the person of the Lord Jesus. Even though he was God, he willingly came to earth and became a servant. He stooped down to wash the feet of his disciples. When others refused to even travel through the region of the detested Samaritans, the compassionate Lord Jesus went there and loved them (John 4). He was not afraid of getting dirty by ministering to people of the street. While others lifted up their proud noses high in the air and passed by, the Lord Jesus stooped down to heal and save. He willingly suffered the rebuke and scorn of those around him. He did not hesitate to go to the cross to die for those who were his enemies. He had a servant's heart. He did not claim his rights as the Lord of the universe. He willingly set aside his divine privileges and human comforts and considered others to be more important than himself. Paul challenged the Ephesians to adopt the same humble attitude as their Lord.

Pride is a terrible sin. This was the sin that caused the fall of Satan and his angels. Pride will not listen to correction. It places itself above others and has no other objective in life but to satisfy self. This is contrary to everything that God teaches us in his Word. Human pride is a barrier between people and God and blocks his full blessing.

Be Gentle (verse 2)

Paul also challenged the Ephesians to be gentle. Gentleness is, in many ways, the outworking of the attitude of humility. While humility is the attitude of the heart, gentleness is the response of the humble heart to those around it. Gentleness comes from a heart that does not want to hurt others. The gentle person will carefully weigh words and actions to be sure that these are uplifting and encouraging, rather than destructive and discouraging. Gentleness treats its brother or sister with love and compassion. It will not force itself on another but guards the dignity of those it meets. Coming from a heart of humility, gentleness responds in love and kindness. It reaches out to bring healing and blessing wherever it goes.

Be Patient with Each Other and Bear with Each Other in Love (verse 2)

True humility will also be patient with others. The Greek word used here is "*makrothumia.*" This word is comprised of two words meaning to go a long time under the wrath or fierceness of another. Patience implies struggle. The person who is patient is willing to suffer for the well-being of others. Patient people will not retaliate when someone does them wrong. They will not abandon the ones they love. They will forgive and persevere in loving gentleness toward others, despite great aggression against them. They do not expect perfection but work with the faults of others.

Keep the Unity of the Spirit (verse 3)

One of the ministries of the Holy Spirit is to create unity in the body of Christ. Where the Holy Spirit is working there is wonderful unity. Where the Spirit of God is at work disagreements seem to melt, anger and resentment are calmed, and forgiveness is sought. Old hostilities are broken in the name of the Lord Jesus and relationships are restored. The Holy Spirit seems to delight in restoring relationships and bringing peace and unity to the body of Christ. That unity, however, can be destroyed if we begin to nurture the sinful flesh. It is possible for us to resist the work of the Holy Spirit and instead allow the works of the flesh to flourish in us.

Paul's challenge to the Ephesians here was that they die to the selfish cravings of the flesh and allow the Spirit of God to create unity among them. They were to be bound together with the cords of peace. This is the peace that comes from reconciliation with our brothers and sisters. It comes when we willingly forgive those who have offended us, even as the Lord Jesus forgave us. This unity does not mean that we are all the same. We can be very different and yet be of one mind and love for Christ and each other. The challenge of Paul to the Ephesians was that they work hard to maintain unity in the church of Christ.

Paul concluded this part of his challenge by reminding the Ephesians of things they enjoyed together as believers in Christ. In verses 4–6 Paul reminded them of the oneness they already shared. Paul listed particular areas of oneness.

One Body

As believers in the Lord Jesus, the Ephesians had been set free from the world's way of thinking and placed in the family of God. This family spans time, culture, and denominational affiliation. This was a gentle reminder to the Ephesians that Jews and Gentiles were without distinction in the one church. Paul wanted the Ephesians to lift up their eyes to understand that they were part of something bigger than themselves and their own local fellowship. They were part of a body of believers that spanned time and geography.

No matter where we believers go on this earth, we can find others who belong to the same spiritual body as we do because they too have accepted the Lord Jesus as their Savior. If we are part of the same family, why should we be competing against each other? The success or failure of our sister church down the road is also our success or failure. How we need to see in our day local fellowships that accept each other as part of the same body. While we may not always do things in the same way, if we have accepted the Lord Jesus as our Savior, we are all part of the same body. To bite and devour each other is to bite and devour ourselves.

One Spirit

Not only are we all part of the same body, but there is only one Spirit who leads us all into a deeper intimacy and fellowship with the Lord Jesus Christ. This Spirit works in the church and in each believer for a common goal. We are united in the body of Christ by the Holy Spirit of God.

One Hope

No matter how we express our worship or how we live out our commitment to the Lord Jesus, we share one hope. That hope is that one day the Lord Jesus will return to this earth to bring all God's children to live in his presence forever. We all have one hope of forgiveness through the blood of the Lord Jesus. We all know one hope of heaven and eternal life with the Lord Jesus who died for us on the cross. This common hope unites us as believers.

One Lord

We also serve one Lord. While we may serve or worship him in different ways, our focus is nonetheless on the Lord Jesus as the Head of the church. It should bring delight to our hearts to see our brothers and sisters in the faith worshiping and serving the Lord Jesus all over this globe. Any glory that goes to our one Lord ought to rejoice our hearts.

One Faith

While we may not all agree on minor doctrinal issues, we all believe that the Lord Jesus, the Son of God, came to this earth to die for sinners. We believe that he left us his Word and his Holy Spirit to guide us into truth. We believe that he offers salvation to all who accept his death on their behalf. We also believe that he will return to take those who belong to him to heaven and to condemn to eternal damnation those who have refused his sacrifice. In these matters of faith, we are united as believers.

One Baptism

There is also, said Paul, only one baptism. The practice of the early church was to baptize those who came to faith in the Lord Jesus. That baptism was done in the name of the Father, Son, and the Holy Spirit and symbolized a believer's entrance into the kingdom of God. While all the disciples baptized, they did so based on the Lord's work on the cross (Matthew 28:19). The baptism of Paul was the same as the baptism of Peter or Apollos. The symbolism was the same.

Paul made a very similar statement in 1 Corinthians 1:13–14 when he asked: "Is Christ divided? Was Paul crucified for you? Were you baptized into the name of Paul? I am thankful that I did not baptize any of you except Crispus and Gaius." Obviously the issue of baptism was very divisive in those days. If someone was baptized by a certain person, they saw themselves as followers of that person. In a similar way, in our day those who are baptized in a certain denomination see themselves as followers of that denomination. Paul is showing us the foolishness of this way of thinking. We are not baptized in the name of the Baptist or Presbyterian Church; we are baptized in the name of the Lord Jesus. There are not many baptisms but only one. We are all baptized into the Lord Jesus, symbolized by water baptism.

There are those who view the baptism Paul spoke of here as a reference to the baptism of the Spirit. This refers to the Holy Spirit coming to dwell in the lives of believers, enabling them to understand the plan of salvation and giving them new life in Christ. If this is the case, Paul was reminding the Ephesians that there was only one work of the Spirit that brings salvation and spiritual life. Again, this was cause for unity.

One God and Father of All

The basic doctrine taught in all Scripture is that there is only one God and Father. This God and Father is over all. He alone is God. To him we must all bow our knees. We do not bow to our particular doctrinal distinctive. We do not bow to our particular worship style. We bow the knee to the one God and Father who is over all. Anything else is idolatry.

This same God is also through all and in all. We all owe our very existence to this God. Nothing could have been created without him. We owe every beat of our hearts and every breath of our lungs to this one God. Without him we would not exist. We are bound together by the very life he gives to us.

Having said all this, Paul challenged the believers of Ephesus to realize that they had much in common with each other (whether Jew or Gentile). Instead of focusing on their differences and fighting with each other over those differences, they needed to band together in love and humility and realize that they were brothers and sisters in the same family. They were all members of the same team competing for the same goal—to bring glory to God. May we strive for unity in the church of our day as well.

For Consideration:

- Do you have the humility and gentleness toward your brother and sister that Paul spoke about in this section? How could this attitude be more clearly demonstrated in your life?

- Why do you suppose we see so much division among true believers of our day? What particularly divides us as believers?

- What united the Ephesians with other believers?

- Does your church have concern for sister churches in your community? How does your church demonstrate unity of the body of Christ to your community?

For Prayer:

- Take a moment to praise the Lord for another church in your community. What evidence of God's blessing is there in this church? Thank the Lord for that blessing.

- Ask God to break down the barriers that have risen against unity in the body of Christ.

- Ask God to give you a deeper concern for the body of Christ. Ask him to give you a humble and gentle heart like Jesus for those around you.

- Thank God that you are part of the body of Christ. Ask God to help you to love all who are in his spiritual body.

19

He Gave Gifts to Men

Read Ephesians 4:7–16

In the last meditation, the apostle Paul challenged the Ephesians to strive toward unity in the body of Christ. He reminded them of all the spiritual realities they had in common as believers. In this next section, he gave yet another reason why they needed to strive toward unity in the body of Christ. In verse 7 Paul reminded them that, as believers, they had each received a special measure of grace. The Greek word for "grace" that Paul used here is *"charis."* This is the same word he used when speaking about the spiritual gifts that God had distributed to the body in Romans 12 and 1 Corinthians 12. It is obvious from the context that Paul was speaking here about the spiritual gifts the Lord had given them (see verse 11).

Paul told the Ephesians that Christ had given to each member of his body a special gift, enabling each believer to play a unique role in the church. We need each other if we are going to function as God intended. God has created the church in such a way that the members are interdependent. This is a practical incentive for seeking unity and the means by which it can be attained. Without this harmony and organization, the body of Christ will be chaotic and weak. The apostle used a passage from Psalm 68 as a picture of our Lord ascending to heaven, leading captives in his train, and giving gifts to his people. The picture painted here is of a conquering commander returning home with a parade of enemies bound and chained behind him. There is great praise and rejoicing as the people line the roads, watching their conquering king return.

This is what the Lord Jesus did for us. He came to earth and engaged in spiritual battle against the enemies of heaven. By his death on the cross, he conquered those enemies and returned to heaven a victorious warrior. There is another important part of this picture that we need to see. As the conquering warrior returns with the enemies following behind, he showers his people with the riches he has acquired from his defeated foes. Similarly, we too have received gifts from the Lord Jesus because of his victory over the enemy. These gifts are not physical in nature but spiritual.

In verse 9 Paul told the Ephesians that for this victory to be possible, Christ Jesus had to descend to the lower earthly regions. This can be confusing. What did Paul mean when he said that Christ descended to the lower earthly regions? There are several possibilities. First, there are those who say that this reference to the lower parts of the earth simply means that the Lord Jesus was willing to leave heaven and come to earth to give us victory over sin and Satan. Others believe that this phrase refers to the grave. In order to obtain victory over Satan and sin, the Lord Jesus died on the cross and descended into the lowest parts of the earth, that is to say, he was buried in the tomb.

Another proposal is that the phrase is referring to hell, when Jesus went to preach the gospel to those imprisoned spirits who had disobeyed during the days of Noah (1 Peter 3:18–20). Still others see a reference to the descent of the Lord Jesus into God's holy wrath because of our sins. Christ conquered sin by taking on a human body and living a perfect life among sinners. He conquered death by dying for sin and then rising victoriously on the third day. He conquered Satan by facing him directly and experiencing his temptations all through his earthly life.

However we interpret the phrase, we are led to one final conclusion: Jesus conquered sin, Satan, death, and hell. As he returned to his Father in heaven, all these foes were bound, chained, and followed behind him as he paraded his victory through the streets of glory. Because of his wonderful and complete victory, he returned to heaven to dwell high above any creature. His glory now fills the entire world. Even the gates of hell have been forced to surrender to his lordship.

It was this conquering Jesus who gave a variety of gifts to his church. Paul listed five of these gifts in this section. While they are rightfully called gifts, we can see them as different offices in the church. Let us briefly look at these various offices given by Christ as gifts to the church.

Apostles

The first of these offices mentioned is that of apostles. This was the role that God had called Paul to fulfill in the church. There were twelve other apostles (Matthias was chosen to replace Judas in Acts 1:12–23). They were called of God as founders of the church. They were gifted in a very particular way to pass on the truth that the Lord Jesus had given them. One of the qualifications for being an apostle was that the candidates needed to have physically been with Jesus while he was on this earth. They also had to be witnesses of his resurrection (see Acts 1:22). The early church based their teaching on the teachings of the apostles as it was accurately passed on through them from the Lord Jesus and the Spirit of God (see Acts 2:42). This was a very particular calling indeed. If some recognize an office of apostle today, it could never be on the same level as the specific calling of apostle in the days of the early church.

Prophets

The second offices in the early church was that of prophets. The role of prophets was to bring the Word to God's people. They spoke for God. The vast majority of prophecy in the Scripture is not a prediction of the future but rather a specific word of God to the day in which it was spoken. Prophets were particularly gifted of God to speak his word to the culture in which they lived. They differed from teachers in that their major concern was not systemic instruction in the Scriptures but speaking the revealed word of God into current situations.

Surely these individuals are still needed in the body of Christ today. Under the inspiration of the Holy Spirit, they bring conviction of sin, comfort, encouragement, and edification to the church by means of the spoken word the Lord puts on their hearts (see 1 Corinthians 14:3). It should be mentioned here, however, that the word of any prophetic preacher or teacher is subject to the inspired words of God in the Bible. Any prophetic word that does not line up perfectly with the Scripture must be rejected as false, along with the person who spoke it.

Evangelists

The third office mentioned here is the office of evangelist. Very clearly the office of evangelist has to do with proclaiming the truth of the gospel to those who are still in their sins. These individuals are gifted of God to proclaim the simple message of salvation in such a way that men and women respond to that message and commit their lives to the Savior. This is a very essential gift for the continued growth of the body of Christ.

Pastors

The fourth office given to the church is the office of pastor. The role of the pastor is to care for a specific group of believers. He does this in many different ways. The pastor protects the sheep from harm, nurses them to health when they are wounded, and provides ongoing spiritual nourishment for their continued growth in the Lord. The pastor most often cares for a local group of individuals. The pastor's role is the most varied of all the offices in that if he is to care for his flock, he must exercise a variety of roles (evangelist, teacher, counselor, and administrator). His major concern is to care for a select group of believers.

Teachers

The final office mentioned here is the office of teacher. The role of teacher is to expound the truth of the Scriptures so that God's Word can be understood and applied to life in general. The difference between a prophet and a teacher is that when people sit under the ministry of a teacher, they gain a deep appreciation of the Scriptures and a deeper appreciation of the God who inspired those Scriptures. When they sit under a prophet, they are convicted of particular sins or comforted in a specific situation they are going through at the time. The teachers keep us true to the Word of God and its requirements. They give us clear understanding of what the Scriptures teach and keep us from falling into error.

In verse 12 Paul reminded the Ephesians of the reason why the Lord gave these offices to the church. These offices equip the body of Christ for works of service. These gifted individuals are not given to the church so that others can sit back and watch them work. They are given to the church to help others serve the Lord. It is the responsibility of the whole church to serve interdependently. The role of the apostles, prophets, evangelists, pastors, and teachers is to help believers to excel in their unique spiritual gifts for the good of all.

Paul told the Ephesians that the work of equipping each other would not be over until they reached unity in faith and knowledge of the Lord Jesus and until they became mature in him and knew the whole measure of his fullness. In other words, as long as there is a corner of our lives that does not know the fullness of the Lord Jesus, there is still work to do. As long as there are brothers and sisters who have not come to full understanding of what the Lord Jesus has really done for them and wants to do through them, then we still have ministry to do. Our labor will not be over until each one of us reaches maturity in the Lord Jesus. Is it not very clear that there is still much work to do?

When these offices or gifts are properly exercised, there are several things that happen in the body.

We Will No Longer Be Infants Tossed Back and Forth (verse 14)

The world in which we live is filled with its pagan philosophies and ideals. The church of our day is not sheltered from these pagan ways or from false teachings that slip into the church by the trickery of cunning schemers. Even strong believers can feel the pull of these crafty plots. How many times have we watched brothers and sisters move from Christ and back to the world? One moment they are on fire for the Lord, and the next moment they are turning their backs on him in their families and work places. The Lord has placed within the body the gifts necessary for believers to mature in biblical thinking and living. Through the use of these spiritual gifts, God intends that his infant children mature in faith, not easily confused but given strength to stand firm against the winds of worldly ideas and perverted doctrines.

We Will Grow Up into Him Who Is the Head (verse 15)

All of these offices and gifts have as their function to draw us closer to the Lord Jesus and to mature us to be like him. By being committed to truth and love in speech and conduct, the whole church comes to know the Lord in a much deeper, more intimate way. Jesus becomes more real to us, and we grow in knowledge and devotion to him. God is reproducing in his children the truthful and loving character of his dear Son.

We Will Be United in the Effort of Building Up the Body in Love (verse 16)

Finally, Paul told the Ephesians that when these gifts were properly exercised in the body of Christ, they would all be united in one effort, building up the body in love. The whole body grows as each part performs its proper function. What a wonderful thing it is to see the body of Christ at work in this way. Each member is deeply concerned and watching out for the other. Each member is building up and encouraging others. This is a powerful witness to the world around us. When the world sees how we love and care for each other, they may realize that the Lord is with us. How wonderful it is to be part of such a loving and growing community.

For Consideration:

- What did Paul tell the Ephesians that God had done for them?

- Has the Lord given you a leadership role in the church? Which spiritual gifts has he given you to use for the good of the larger body?

- Who are the people God has used to mature you in the faith? Which gifts were they using?

For Prayer:

- Consider for a moment the local church where you attend. To what extent does this church show maturity and unity in Christ? Take a moment to pray for your church.

- Which spiritual gifts are exhibited in your local church? Which gifts or offices appear to be missing?

- Thank God for the gifts he has given you and your local church, and pray that he will send you people who have other gifts.

20

Putting On the New Self

Read Ephesians 4:17–32

I t is clear from this letter to the Ephesians that the Lord gives gifts to the church in order that it might be built up in love and spiritual maturity. In light of this fact, Paul challenged the Ephesians in this next section to cooperate with what the Lord wanted to do in them by taking off their old sinful nature and putting on their new pure nature.

Paul insisted "in the Lord" that the Ephesians stop living like the Gentiles (verse 17). We need to understand that many of the people to whom the apostle was writing were Gentile believers. When Paul used the term "Gentile," he was not speaking about nationality but was referring to unbelievers. Paul told the Ephesian believers that they were not to live like unbelievers. There was to be a difference between the saved and the unsaved. When the unbelieving world looked at the Ephesian Christians, they were to see a very clear difference in the way they thought and acted.

Paul told the Ephesians that the thoughts of the unbelieving world are empty and without meaning. In verses 18–19 Paul described this unbelieving way of thinking.

They Are Darkened in Their Understanding (verse 18)

What understanding did you have, as an unbeliever, of the joy of the Lord? How much excitement did you find in the Word of God or the worship of his name? Before the Holy Spirit came to live in our hearts, we lived in the dark. We had no real concept of spiritual matters. The things of God did not make sense to us. We could not understand a believer's desire for the Lord and his ways. All this changed the day we came to know the Lord Jesus as our Savior. It was as though his glorious light penetrated our hearts and darkness left. All of a sudden there was an understanding of spiritual things we never had before.

They Are Separated from the Life of God (verse 18)

Unbelievers are separated from God in their hearts and lives. The difference between the believer and the unbeliever is the presence of God. The life and presence of God flows through the believer by the Holy Spirit. But there is a separation between the ungodly unbeliever and the holy Lord. Sin forms an invisible barrier between God and unsaved people. That barrier can only be broken by faith in the redeeming death of the Lord Jesus and the forgiveness he offers. Unbelievers can have no communion or relationship with truth, love, and holiness, and this is reflected in their thoughts and actions.

They Have Lost All Sensitivity (verse 19)

Because the unbelieving heart is hardened to the things of God, it is insensitive to spiritual matters. The unsaved are hardened by their sins, and they fight against morality, kindness, and purity. They are blind and deaf to the beauty and truth of God. The unbelieving heart does not hear God, and its senses are dead to the matters of the Spirit.

They Have Given Themselves Over to Sensuality (verse 19)

The unbelieving heart is not motivated by the moral will of God. But if unbelievers do not live for God, what do they live for? Paul told the Ephesians that unsaved people are given over to sensuality. What is sensuality? It is the pleasing of the flesh. Selfish desires motivate the actions of unbelievers. They indulge in those things that will bring them pleasure in life. They do not function on a spiritual level, but rather on a physical and emotional level that continually lusts for more.

Paul challenged the Ephesians to put away this mentality (verses 20–22). He encouraged them to cast this unbelieving way of thinking far from them because of the truth they knew about the Lord Jesus. As believers, they were to live above their old way of thinking because they had been saved from its deceitful lusts, which promise satisfaction but end in futility.

How easy it is for us to get trapped into the worldly way of thinking. In our materialistic and pleasure-seeking society, we are being bombarded constantly with the lusts of the world. We are told to live life to the full by indulging the appetites of the flesh. Christ, on the other hand, calls us to die to selfish desires. Not every believer is willing to put aside the strong motivations of sin. There are many believers who love the world too much.

Paul told the Ephesians in verses 23 and 24 that when they put off the old way of thinking, two things would happen.

They Would Be Made New in Their Attitude (verse 23)

As long as we cling to the things of the world, we will never experience a renewing of our minds. In order for our minds to become more like Christ, we need to cut off the world's entrance into our thoughts. How do we expect to have the mind of Christ and his attitude in us if we continue to soak up the world's way of thinking? Putting off the old self implies spending less time entertaining ourselves in ways that do not glorify the Lord Jesus. It implies spending more time in the Word of God.

When we begin to focus our attention on the things of God and not on the world, we will see a tremendous progression of change in our attitudes. The things that used to entertain will gradually lose their attraction. The more we focus on the person and redemptive work of the Lord Jesus, the more we will understand his power and beauty, and the less we will be connected to the cares and concerns of this world. The minds of many are not being renewed because they are willfully exposing themselves to the philosophies and ideals of this world. But when we begin to put off the old self with all its ideas, we will soon discover that God is renewing our minds into the image of Christ.

They Would Be Clothed with True Righteousness and Holiness (verse 24)

The second thing that will happen when we take responsibility to live according to the truth of the Word of God is that we will begin to discover that not only are our minds being renewed but also our whole being. With pure thoughts comes a whole new self. Our attitudes and actions are transformed. Our lust for sin can only grow if we feed it. When we die to sin and the old lusts of the flesh, they wither away in us. As we resist the enemy, he flees from us (James 4:7). Our whole being is transformed. We are no longer the same. Our life becomes more righteous and holy.

Paul was not promoting a religion of works here. He was saying that victory in the Christian life will only come by grace through faith as we humbly surrender and commit ourselves to putting on the new self. Only by obedience do we labor with the Spirit of God to transform our lives. Paul is encouraging us here to cooperate with what God is already doing in our lives in the new self he created in us.

In light of this, Paul exhorted the Ephesians in specific ways to change their conduct (verses 25–32). First, they were to stop lying and speak only truth. Honesty is necessary for the church to function in peace. Lying includes such things as exaggeration, cheating, foolish promises, and false excuses.

Second, they were to resist the temptation to sin when angry (verse 26). There is an anger that hates injustice and immorality, and there is an anger that comes when selfish desires are thwarted. But even righteous anger can turn to bitterness if it is not dealt with quickly. Paul recommended that they set aside their anger by the end of each day so as not to give Satan a foothold in their hearts and in their church.

There is no telling what will happen when Satan succeeds in planting bitterness or wrath in our hearts. Whole churches have been destroyed because of someone giving Satan an open door into his or her life. Testimonies have been ruined, believers have wandered away from the fold, and the name of Christ has been blasphemed because people have not dealt with their anger. We cannot allow Satan this opportunity. By dealing with our anger, we can actively resist him.

Third, the Ephesians were to stop abusing the property of others (verse 28). Those who stole were to start working hard to earn their living. God honors hard, honest, honorable work by blessing it so that workers have something to share with those who have physical needs.

Fourth, they were to refuse to let any unholy words come out of their mouths (verse 29). Instead, they were to determine to speak only those things that encouraged and guided others in the proper direction. All bitterness, rage, anger, brawling, slander, and malice were to be replaced by kindness, compassion, and forgiveness (verses 31–32).

Notice in verse 30 that if we do not die to self and put off the old ways of the flesh, we will grieve the Holy Spirit of God. What does this mean? This reminds us that the Holy Spirit has personhood. He personally cares for believers and is their indwelling guarantor of eternal redemption. When the Holy Spirit is grieved, he pulls back his blessing and empowering in our lives. When this happens our ministry becomes powerless. When he is grieved, Christians begin to live in defeat. When the children of Israel grieved God in the Old Testament, sometimes the enemy came in and took over. They were helpless to defeat their enemies and lost the sense of the presence of God. They were left barren and dry. They could no longer enjoy the things of God because they had driven his Holy Spirit from them.

As children of God, we need to grow in the self-control of putting off the old self. We are to realize that we are now new creatures in Christ and, as such, no longer live according to our former ways. As his children, we should commit ourselves to zealously live for him and do his will. This will take a very definite effort on our part. By putting off the old ways, we resist Satan and give place for the Holy Spirit of God to work in our lives. We will be renewed in our minds and live according to God in true righteousness and holiness.

For Consideration:

- Are there any ways that you are still allowing the enemy to influence your thinking and your actions?

- What difference did the Lord Jesus make in your life when he saved you?

- In what way do you feel the temptation to be like the world? Where are you most easily tempted by the enemy?

- What does this section teach us about the effort we need to make if we are to become the children God has called us to be?

- What is the difference between a religion of works and a disciplined life of godliness?

For Prayer:

- Ask the Lord to reveal to you any ways in which you have given the enemy a foothold in your life. Ask him to give you victory over these wicked attitudes.

- Ask God to fill you afresh with his Spirit and a real desire to seek after Christ in your life.

- Ask God to help you to willingly put aside anything that hinders the work of God's Holy Spirit in your life.

21

Living in the Light

Read Ephesians 5:1–21

Paul had reminded the Ephesians of their spiritual condition before they came to know the Lord Jesus as their Savior. And now that they belonged to Christ, their behavior needed to reflect their new life in the Spirit. Paul had stated that the Ephesians were to put off their old selfish ways and live as children of God. He had called them to unity, and holiness, and next he called them to love.

As children of God, the Ephesians were to be imitators of their heavenly Father (verse 1). As his children, their lives were to reflect his love—even as the Lord Jesus declared the Father's love by coming to earth and dying as a sacrifice to God for his chosen ones (verse 2). When the Lord Jesus came to this earth, he committed himself to obeying his Father even to death. Christ's death was a fragrant aroma to his heavenly Father, completely satisfying his divine wrath. Paul expected the Ephesians to take as their example of love the person of the Lord Jesus. If he, as the Lord of the universe, lovingly surrendered his life for them, how could they do any less for him?

We are to follow in Christ's footsteps. How would you characterize your relationship with your brothers and sisters in the Lord? Do you live a sacrificial lifestyle? Do you, like the Lord Jesus, willingly surrender your rights for the welfare of others? How is your relationship with God? Would you willingly sacrifice your life in obedience to him? Would you lay down your life as did your Savior in order to show the love of God? Would you risk your reputation? Would you swallow your pride to advance God's kingdom?

Notice that Paul taught the Ephesians that there ought not even to be a "hint" of the perversion of love among them (verse 3). In other words, the believer should be so far removed from the practice of sin that even the smallest trace of it would be immediately sought out and dealt with before it infected the rest of the body. In an age of compromise, the church of our day needs to take this verse seriously. We cannot flirt with the world and its desires. We must flee from even the smallest evidence of immorality. How tempting it is to take a peek or to linger for a moment before turning our backs. Paul is telling us here that believers ought to flee the moment they see any hint of sin.

Paul listed some of the sins that the Ephesians needed to beware of in verses 3–5. He challenged them to flee from any hint of sexual immorality or uncleanness. This includes any form of sexual sin. Unfaithfulness in marriage, sexual relations before marriage, and pornography all fall under these types of sin.

Immorality is closely associated with greed (verse 3). Greed is an unhealthy lust for possessions. While it is not wrong to enjoy the good things the Lord has given us, there are times when the enjoyment of good things turns to lust. At this point we begin to hold tightly to our possessions. The accumulation of this world's goods becomes an end in itself. We become dissatisfied with the things the Lord has given us and desire more and more. At times our lust for possessions may keep us from doing what is right. People in our lives may begin to suffer as we become absorbed in the pursuit of things. How easy it is in our materialistic society to get caught up in the pursuit of more of what we already have enough of.

Paul moved on to speak of the sins of the tongue (verse 4). We need also to flee from any hint of obscenity, foolish talk, and course joking. All of these things are out of place for the believer. How often do we hear the unbeliever laughing at sin and immorality? How many immoral jokes circulate in our work places and schools? Sin is not a laughing matter. Immorality and lust are not things to laugh about. Greed and covetousness are terrible things in the eyes of God, and to laugh at the practice of these sins is to mock the God who detests them. Remember that the Lord Jesus came to die in order to set us free from these practices. The heart of the believer should be broken by these sins, even as God's heart is broken. Be assured that any words that come from our mouths that treat sin as something to laugh at do not come from the Spirit of God.

The words spoken by the believer ought to be words seasoned with the salt of thanksgiving (verse 4). Everything that the believer says should be from a heart of gratitude and praise to God for all his blessings. Are the words you speak from a heart of love and filled with holy thanksgiving and praise?

Paul reminded the Ephesians that no immoral, impure, or greedy person has a place in the kingdom of God (verse 5). There is no place in the kingdom of God for these sins and those who practice them. Those whose hearts are given over to these practices prove that they do not belong to God. Those who belong to God are ashamed of these activities.

If our lives consist of the pursuit of the pleasures and possessions of this world, what proof do we have that we belong to God? Those who belong to God have experienced a change in their lives. Jesus came to set us free from these sins. His Spirit within us brings conviction of these sins. We should be repulsed by those things that are an abomination to God. To actively pursue these sins is to make possessions and pleasures of this life a god. This is idolatry. We cannot serve two gods. If we are serving the god of this world who hates us, we are not serving the true God who loves us.

It appears that there were those who were trying to water down the truth about judgment of sin (verse 6). Paul told the Ephesians that the wrath of God would fall on those who ignored the truth of his Word and lived in disobedience. The Ephesians were not to participate in any wickedness so they would avoid the discipline of God.

Even in the churches of our land, we see a watering down of the basic truths about morality and godliness. We cannot afford to lower our standards simply because the world around us does. Paul told the Ephesians in verse 7 to have nothing to do with anyone who lived in disobedience. It is wrong for the objects of God's love to participate in sin with those who are the object of God's wrath.

Paul told them to not live anymore as darkness (verse 8). Jesus had set them free from being darkness. They were to live as light in the Lord and evidence the fruit of light: goodness, righteousness, and truth. If our actions do not pass the test of goodness, righteousness, and truth, then we should flee from these activities and expose them as being from the enemy (verse 11). Notice that it is the sin we should flee from and not necessarily the sinner, who needs salvation.

Paul told the Ephesians in verse 12 that it is shameful to even speak about those things that wicked people do in secret. Paul already told the Ephesians in verse 4 that they were not to joke about sin and evil. Here in verse 12 he told them that they should even avoid speaking about the evil deeds practiced in the world. To speak of these evil deeds would be to linger on them and draw attention to them.

Paul was saying that believers should not even allow their minds to be polluted with the thoughts and pictures of what sinners do in secret. Certainly this would include some things we see on our televisions and movies of our day. We belong to God, and our bodies are his temple. We shouldn't allow our minds to focus on wicked deeds. We should recognize them as being of the flesh and of the devil and flee from them. Better yet, we should keep away from those places where we are exposed to evil.

Paul told the Ephesians to bring everything to the light of God (verse 13). The fruit of darkness will become clear when it is exposed to the light of God's Word (verse 14). One day God will make all things visible, and he will expose the secrets of sin. Paul challenged the believers in Ephesus to wake from any ungodly lifestyles and let the light of Christ shine on any dark recesses of their hearts.

This same challenge goes out to us in our day. How we need to wake up to the reality of how much darkness we have been letting into our lives. Paul warns us to wisely examine how we live and how we spend our time. How many hours do we waste on the passing things of this world? How much time do we spend filling our minds with impure thoughts? These are evil days in which we live (verse 16). The darkness of Satan is penetrating into the lives of believers. This is a time to take action and stand firm in the light of Christ. This is a time to energize our hearts and minds with the truth and love of God so that we can stand against the flood of darkness. Life is short, and we should take every opportunity for worship and service.

Paul made some suggestions in verses 17–20 as to how believers can fill their hearts and minds with light and truth. First, he said not to be drunk with wine but rather be filled and controlled by the Spirit of God (verse 18). Let the Holy Spirit of God have control of every aspect of your life and live consciously in his presence. Don't grieve him but learn to surrender to his leading and guidance. Learn what his voice sounds like by reading Scripture. Depend on his power for every pure thought and good deed. Welcome his light and truth into every part of your life as your ongoing responsibility.

Second, Paul said to speak to each other with psalms, hymns, and spiritual songs (verse 19). When the Spirit is in control of your life, you will be joyful. You should surround yourself with other believers and join with them in praise and thanksgiving of the one true God for his grace, love, and salvation. Let the praise of God fill your heart and drive out the evil thoughts of darkness. Fill your mind and mouth with holy worship and praise of God.

Third, give thanks to the Lord your God for everything that comes your way (verse 20). When the Spirit is in control, you will be thankful. Stop complaining and grumbling. Realize that God has promised to use everything in your life for good. Don't let the enemy fill your mind with negative and bitter thoughts. Don't doubt the goodness of God. Instead, be thankful. Cultivate an attitude of gratitude even in the most trying times. The desire of the enemy is to plunge you into the darkness of doubt and complaint. Don't give in to evil. Fight this darkness with the light of thanksgiving and praise to God. Be confident in him and trust his plan.

Finally, resist the darkness by submitting to one another out of reverence to Christ (verse 21). When the Spirit is in control of your life, you will be humble in your relationships. You are not alone in this battle against darkness. God has made you part of his family. As a member of this family, you are to watch out for others. When your brother or sister warns you about the darkness, listen to what he or she has to say. Don't be so proud that you cannot listen to the warnings of another. Submit your life, as did Christ, to the good of others and the glory of God.

For Consideration:

- Are there any areas of your life where you are allowing the darkness of the world to filter into your thoughts and actions? What are they?

- How can we help each other as believers to fight the darkness of this world as it seeks entrance into our own hearts and churches?

- Take a moment to examine your speech patterns. Do you speak from a heart of thanksgiving and praise?

- Have you ever found yourself lingering for a moment on sin? What does Paul tell us about this in this passage?

For Prayer:

- Ask the Lord to give you more of his heart. Ask him to help you to see sin as he sees it.

- Do you know of a believer who is caught up in the pursuit of the things of this world? Take a moment now to pray that the Lord would set this person free.

- Ask the Lord to help you to make better use of your time so you can fill you heart and mind with the light of his Word.

- Thank God for brothers and sisters in Christ who can help us in the battle against sin.

22

Husbands and Wives

Read Ephesians 5:22–33

ere in this next section, the apostle Paul turned his attention to the relationship between husband and wife. Let us consider the general principles Paul addressed regarding marriage in this passage.

Wives, Submit to Your Husbands (verses 22–24)

This word "submit" has many different definitions in our day. It has been used and abused by men in all ages. What did Paul mean when he told the wife to submit to her husband?

Before we examine this in any detail, it is important to see that Paul challenged the wife to submit to her husband "as to the Lord." There are two ways of understanding this phrase. First, we can understand it to mean that the wife is to submit to her husband for the sake of the Lord, seeing that this is the Lord's will for her. It is clearly taught in the Scriptures that the husband is to be the head of the home (Colossians 3:18; 1 Peter 3:5–6). The wife, by accepting his leadership, submits to the will of the Lord. She does this for the Lord and in agreement with his purpose for marriage.

There is a second way of looking at this phrase "as unto the Lord." The wife is to submit to her husband in the same way she submits to the Lord. How do we submit to the Lord? We offer ourselves to him as a living sacrifice. Paul was encouraging wives to do the same thing for their husbands. Wives are to offer their lives to their husbands as a living sacrifice. We submit to the Lord for life. We promise to be faithful to him even unto death. In the same way, the wife is to be faithful to her husband even unto death.

Why should the wife submit to her husband? Paul went on to say in verse 23 that the husband is, by God's design, the head of the wife even as Christ is the head of the church. The wife needs to submit to her husband's leadership role so that their marriage can be a reflection of the church submitting to Christ's leadership role. We live in a God-ordered world in which there is leadership and submission at every level of society.

How does Christ exercise his headship in the church? As spiritual head, the Lord Jesus came to earth in the form of a man to serve humanity. As head, he willingly suffered the insults and cruelties of humanity for us. He offered his life and died for us on the cross. He bore our sins in his body on the cross and suffered separation from God because of those sins. The Bible portrays the Lord Jesus as one who served humankind in every way. He set an example for husbands to follow in marriage. Christ's headship was exercised in sacrificial love for the body. He did not come to lord it over us but chose rather to bow down and wash our feet. He leads by example.

Paul told husbands that their headship is to be like the headship of Christ. In exercising this role of headship, they are to become their wives' greatest servants. They are to live their lives with their wives' needs in view. They are to expend their efforts and their energies, even as Christ did for them, reaching out in loving service to their wives. Those who dominate women or consider them inferior are not following the example of Christ. Headship is not dictatorship. Headship is not being *boss*. Headship is about service and ministry to those who are under our authority.

Having said this, there is no doubt that, while the Lord Jesus reached down to wash our feet, he was still Lord. Just because he adopted the role of servant did not mean that the church was then excused from following his headship. On the contrary, his service to the body made him an even better leader. He could identify with the needs of the body. The best leaders are those who understand their followers. Jesus experienced the things we face in this earthly life (see Hebrews 2:17–18; 4:15). Husbands who properly exercise a servant headship gain the respect of their wives and a willing submission to that headship.

Paul told the wives in verse 24 to submit to the headship of their husbands in all things. Admittedly, this is much easier when the husband is exercising a Christ-like headship. Notice that Paul told the wives to be submissive in "everything." It should be understood that this does not apply to those things that are contrary to the clear teaching of the Word of God. When faced with a decision of whether to obey a husband in participating in evil, the wife, obviously, needs to obey the Lord instead. The example of Sapphira's personal accountability makes this clear (Acts 5:9). A wife should protect herself and her children from danger.

The word *everything* implies that the submission of the wife is in all aspects of her life and marriage. It may be possible to be submissive in certain areas of life and not in others. According to Paul, the wife needs to cultivate an attitude of dying to self for the building up of her marriage and her spiritual maturity. Even as she willingly surrenders to the will of Christ in her life, so she should also be willing to surrender to her husband as the God-ordained head of the home.

How often do we find competition in marriage? Marriage can become a battle for personal rights. Remember that in marriage God calls the couple to become one flesh (Genesis 2:24). God did not intend marriage to increase human selfishness. Spouses should not just do things their way and ignore the interests of their partners. Marriage needs to be a blending of minds, gifts, and emotions. This should be reflected in the life and ministry of the couple. Their gifts and talents should complement each other. To increase the success of a marriage, God intends wives to be willing to die to their own interests for the sake of their husbands and for the sake of the kingdom.

Husbands, Love Your Wives (verses 25–31)

It may not be without reason that the apostle Paul, after taking three verses to speak about wives submitting to their husbands, took the next seven verses to speak to husbands about truly loving their wives.

Paul reminded the Ephesian husbands how Christ loved the church and gave himself up for her. He challenged them to imitate Christ's love in their relationships with their wives. They were to remember how Christ willingly offered everything for his church. They were to remember how he died for her. They were to remember how everything he ever did on this earth was for the good of imperfect people. The Ephesian husbands were not to forget how Christ died to himself so that his bride could be lifted up and honored. This was to be their example in loving their wives.

True love is selfless. If husbands love their wives as Christ loved the church, they will always be seeking their wives' purity. Even as the Lord Jesus gave himself so that his bride could become sinless and without corruption (verse 27), so husbands are to make every effort to provide everything their wives need to become all God intended. A husband is not to hold back his wife's spiritual development, but instead to behave in ways that encourage her wholesome service to the King. A husband should make it his delight to see his wife flourish completely—physically, emotionally, socially, and spiritually.

A husband should love his wife as he loves his own body (verse 28). When his body is hungry, he feeds it. When his body is tired, he sees that it gets rest. When his body is sick, he cares for it until it is healed. When I married my wife, I chose before God to become her provider and caregiver. I chose to become one flesh with her. Now it is my responsibility and obligation to provide and care for her in all her needs as I would care for my own needs.

In fact, we husbands are to put our wives' needs before our own, just as the Lord Jesus did for us. What a challenge this verse is for us husbands. How easy it is to live our lives being only concerned for our own needs and not caring for the needs of our spouses. How we need to pray that the Lord would help us to see our spouses as extensions of our own selves. "He who loves his wife loves himself" (verse 28).

Husbands are to nourish and cherish their wives as Christ does the church (verse 29). The Lord takes care of his bride, giving her tender affection so she will be comforted and secure in his love. The church is intimately and inseparably connected to Christ, of his flesh and of his bones (verse 30 NKJV). Even as husband and wife are both to put aside their differences and die to themselves to become one flesh, so God wants the church to experience this same oneness among its members because it is united to Christ.

From the very beginning of time when the Lord instituted marriage, it was his will that the two partners become one flesh (verse 31). Often we see this matter as only being sexual in nature. But this is not the whole truth. Physical oneness is not the oneness that Paul was speaking about here. This oneness has to do with the whole being, physical, emotional, and spiritual. As couples, we are to strive together in the Lord to be permanently unified in all areas of our lives. All areas are important. It is possible to be physically united but not spiritually or emotionally united.

The oneness of the married couple is a symbol of the relationship between Christ and his church. Paul reminded the Ephesians in verse 32 that it is the will of the Father that the church be permanently united with Christ. This is a mystery beyond understanding. How can we ever understand how sinful people could become one with the holy Lord Jesus? Yet this is his desire.

Is your marriage a symbol of this relationship between Christ and the church? Is your marriage a reflection of your personal relationship with Christ? God has created marriage in such a way that only by dying to personal selfishness and by loving and submitting to each other can we experience the oneness that God intended for us to have. Husbands and wives diminish themselves and their testimony for Christ by not attending to the principles stated here for marriage. May the Lord help us to pray for and encourage the marriages in our churches.

For Consideration:

- What are some of the false notions today about submission and headship?

- Has this passage spoken to any particular aspect of your relationship with your spouse? What can you do about it?

- How would you characterize your marriage? Is it characterized by physical, emotional, and spiritual oneness? Which areas of your marriage need work?

- How is marriage a symbol of the relationship between Christ and the church?

For Prayer:

- Ask God to give you a submissive and loving spirit.

- Ask him to help you see your spouse as an extension of your own self so that you care for and minister to your partner as you would for yourself.

- Ask God to give you a heart to seek this oneness with your spouse and with the Lord.

- Ask God to show you in a deeper way how Christ loves his bride. Ask him to give you grace to follow his example more closely.

- Ask the Lord to forgive you for the times you have not respected your partner as God intended.

23

Godly Relationships

Read Ephesians 6:1–9

I n the previous section, the apostle Paul spoke about the relationship that is to exist between a husband and his wife. Here in this next section, Paul dealt with other types of relationships. In verses 1–4 he spoke about the parent-child relationship, and in verses 5–9 he addressed the master-servant relationship. Let's consider these individually.

Parent-Child Relationship

Paul began by speaking to children: "Children, obey your parents in the Lord." Paul made it clear that the child is to obey the parent "in the Lord." The understanding here is that God had been doing a work in the lives of children in Ephesus. They were coming to the Lord and seeking to live godly lives, sometimes in an ungodly family environment. Paul challenged these children to be obedient to their parents in as much as that obedience was in agreement with their greater allegiance to the Lord. In other words, if their parents told them to do something that was not in accordance with the will of God, they were to chose to obey God rather than their parents.

We need to understand that by saying this, the apostle Paul realized that children also have the capacity to make proper spiritual judgments. Even as children, they had the Holy Spirit in their lives. That Holy Spirit can direct a child as easily as he can direct an adult. Let us not underestimate the believing child's capacity to distinguish right from wrong (Proverbs 20:11). Often the Lord uses children as examples to adults.

Not only were children to obey their parents in the Lord but they were also to honor their father and mother. A child can honor a father and mother by having a respectful attitude. When we respect others' positions, we are careful what we say about them and to them. Our respect for them will guard our thoughts and actions concerning them. We will be careful to show the mercy and love of Christ in their time of need.

Notice in verse 2 that Paul told the Ephesians that this was the first commandment of God that actually had a promise attached to it. He quoted this commandment from Exodus 20:12 and Deuteronomy 5:16 where God promised long life in the Promised Land and blessing to those who honored their parents.

What was the nature of this blessing? We are not told. What we need to understand, however, is that when a society loses its respect for parents, chaos and disaster are the natural results. A society that does not show respect for its elders does not show respect for anything else. If our societies fail at the level of the family, they will surely fail at all other levels. When our children do not learn submission to the authority of their parents, they will not respect their teachers in school or any others who are in authority over them. How many problems have begun with disrespect for parental authority? How many criminals come from broken homes? When parents are honored, the society experiences blessing. When children are taught to honor their parents, the crime rate drops and the workplace becomes a much better environment. Not only does the society experience blessing but so does the individual. Some of the most bitter and unhappy people are those who do not respect authority. All this begins at home.

Paul moved on to speak to fathers. He did not mention the mother in this section. He had already mentioned in chapter 5 that the husband is the head of the home. As the leader, it is his responsibility to ensure that discipline is exercised. Paul challenged fathers to not "provoke" (KJV) or "exasperate" (NIV) their children. While discipline is a necessary part of family life, excessive discipline can be devastating for a child. Through unreasonable punishment, a child's spirit can be crushed, driving a child to anger, despair, and resentment. Discipline needs to be exercised with love and concern for each child's uniqueness and feelings. Paul advised against being too stern and dominating.

Fathers are to teach and instruct their children in the ways of the Lord. By lovingly and carefully teaching wisdom from the Word of God, fathers can prevent painful and dangerous situations for their children. Fathers should use every opportunity to lead their children in righteousness, passing on to the next generation the deep truths of Scripture and encouraging them to walk in those truths. This was Paul's advice to fathers in Ephesus. It is his advice to us today as well. While children need to learn obedience and respect, their parents need to be careful not to misuse their authority.

Master-Servant Relationship

While slavery was not something the apostle Paul encouraged, he recognized it as a deeply rooted part of the society in which he lived. The Bible often does speak against the abuses of slavery (Exodus 21:16, 26; Leviticus 25:10; Deuteronomy 23:15–16). Paul taught that believing slaves needed to understand the will of the Lord for their lives. They were to respect their earthly masters. This respect would be demonstrated in how they worked for their masters and how they spoke and thought about them.

Not only were slaves to respect their masters but they were

also to fear them with sincerity of heart. This fear meant reverence and honor for the authority of their masters. Notice that slaves were to do this with sincere hearts. It would be possible for a slave to hate a master and still be obedient and show respect for a master's authority (especially if the master was cruel). Paul reminded slaves that they were to show godly reverence from sincere hearts. They were not to be hypocritical in their relationships with their masters. They were not to obey them simply to win their favor (verse 6). They were to obey their masters as they would obey Christ (verse 5). Paul challenged believing slaves to serve the Lord well by serving their masters well. He reminded them of the heavenly reward they would receive for their faithful service to their earthly masters (verse 8). No good thought or deed will go unrewarded in the age to come.

It should be understood that it was not always easy for a slave to serve a master in this way. Some masters were cruel. Maybe you are in a situation at your work where you feel that you are being treated unfairly. Maybe your boss is not the most understanding person. How should you deal with this situation? You could complain and become bitter. You could demand your rights and fight against those in authority. Paul was saying that believers should have a unique perspective on events in the workplace. When you go to work in the morning, make it your desire to honor the Lord Jesus in how you serve your boss or your company. Commit yourself to respond to your work conditions in a godly and Christ-like way. Work for the Lord, not just for your superiors. You will be amazed to see how much this will transform your attitude in the workplace.

As for the believing masters, Paul told them to treat their slaves with honor and respect. Could it be that Paul realized that there might be a tendency for the believing master to treat a believing slave with more favor than an unbelieving slave? This would only create problems among the slaves.

Paul reminded masters not to take advantage of their authority. They were not to threaten their slaves. They were not to show favoritism. Instead they were to treat them equally and fairly. They were to always remember that both they and their slaves had a common master in heaven. God would not show favoritism. He would not judge them differently because they were masters. All people, both slave and free, will have to give an account of their actions to God. This sobering realization was to govern how they treated their slaves.

For Consideration:

- Paul challenges us in this section to respect any authority over us. Is there evidence of disrespect in your society? Explain.

- How can learning to honor our parents change an entire society?

- Why is it so tempting for those in authority to abuse that authority?

- If you are a parent or a boss at a workplace, how have you used your authority?

- Do you struggle with certain authority figures in your life? What does this passage have to teach you?

For Prayer:

- Ask the Lord to help you to respect and honor those in authority over you.

- Have you ever been guilty of disrespect for authority? Ask the Lord to help you deal with this in your life.

- Have you suffered from the abuse of authority? Ask God to help you to deal with the implications of this in your life. Ask him to bring healing to this part of your life.

- Are you in a position of authority? Ask God to help you to exercise your role with respect for those under you.

24

Be Strong in the Lord

Read Ephesians 6:10

Have you ever wondered what the secret is to victory in the Christian life? Is it possible to live a victorious Christian life with all the temptations and evil that surround us? Let's face it—there isn't one of us who has not failed in his or her walk with the Lord. We have all fallen into the traps of the enemy. We all know believers who seemed to be so strong in their Christian lives but who fell back into the things of the world. There are many things to discourage us in this walk with Christ. Satan and his demons are very real. They are busy opposing the work that God wants to do in our lives.

The apostle Paul understood the nature of the battle as well as anyone. Here in Ephesians 6:10–18 he gave some very important teaching on spiritual warfare. In the course of the next few meditations, we will examine what the apostle Paul taught the Ephesians about overcoming the obstacles and snares that are strewn on the pathway to victorious Christian living.

Paul began this powerful section of Scripture with an introductory statement in verse 10: "Finally, be strong in the Lord and in his mighty power." Let's break this statement into its individual parts and examine them.

Be Strong

Paul told the Ephesians that if they wanted to overcome the enemy and live for the Lord Jesus, they needed to be strengthened. In the original language this phrase "be strong" can be translated "be made strong" or "increase in strength." Paul was saying that if believers want to be overcomers and live the victorious Christian life, they need a strength they do not naturally have.

How often have we tried to win the battle over the world, the flesh, and the devil but failed? Our own strength is not enough. The battle before us is long and hard. The enemy is far more clever and powerful than we are. Satan has had a lot of experience in tempting believers and unbelievers alike. Many before us have fallen into his traps. Among the fallen are those who knew the Bible and had more experience with God than you and I could ever hope to have. Think for a moment of David, the man fully devoted to the Lord. Who would have thought that this godly shepherd boy would fall prey to the temptation to commit adultery and then murder the husband to cover up his sin? Are we above such temptations? Paul tells us in 1 Corinthians 10:12: "So, if you think you are standing firm, be careful that you don't fall!"

If you believe that you are able to handle the temptations of the enemy in your own strength, you are in a very dangerous position. Concerning the church of Laodicea, the Lord Jesus said in Revelation 3:17–18: "You say, 'I am rich; I have acquired wealth and do not need a thing.' But you do not realize that you are wretched, pitiful, poor, blind and naked. I counsel you to buy from me gold refined in the fire, so you can become rich; and white clothes to wear, so you can cover your shameful nakedness; and salve to put on your eyes, so you can see."

Like the church in Laodicea, many people think that they have all it takes to live the Christian life in themselves. Perhaps they simply need a little more discipline and will power. This attitude is an indication of spiritual arrogance. The author of Proverbs tells us in Proverbs 16:18: "Pride goes before destruction, a haughty spirit before a fall." The surest way of falling into spiritual ruin is to think that we can live the life God requires in our own strength. If we want to keep from falling, we need to be made strong.

Do you recognize that you are weak and in need of strength? Do you understand that if you are going to defeat the enemy, you will need strength far greater than your own? Admit it—your enemy is too strong for you. In your own strength you will surely fail. The first step to victory is recognition that you will never be victorious by your own wisdom and power. You must first admit your inability to fight sin and Satan by yourself. You must humbly confess to God your need of his enabling. Only in his strength is victory possible.

Be Strong in the Lord

Notice second in this verse that our strength is to be "in the Lord." What does it mean to be strong in the Lord? Have you ever seen a little brother's boldness when his bigger brother is around? When things get rough, he just runs to his big brother to be safe. The little brother is not strong in himself. His strength is in his big brother.

Being strong in the Lord is very similar. Sometimes we confuse being strong in the Lord with being strong in our knowledge of the Lord or in our experience of the Lord. We can sometimes believe that if we knew enough about Jesus and his ways and had a few years of walking with him, then we would be strong enough to overcome the temptations around us. Enough experience tells us, on the other hand, that even the "spiritual giants" fall. Stories abound of spiritual leaders who have fallen prey to the temptations of the enemy.

Being strong in the Lord is, in reality, like the illustration of the big brother. We can face the enemy not because we know a lot about Jesus and have walked with him for years but because Jesus is right there with us defending and fighting for us. It is his strength and not ours that will win the battle and give us victory. We can know all there is to know about Jesus and fall flat on our faces. We can have real maturity in the Lord and still fall into terrible sin. Victory is not found in our experience of Christ. Victory is only possible when we allow Christ to fight for us.

Listen to what God says to his people in Deuteronomy 20:3–4: "Hear, O Israel, today you are going into battle against your enemies. Do not be fainthearted or afraid; do not be terrified or give way to panic before them. For the LORD your God is the one who goes with you to fight for you against your enemies to give you victory." Notice here that God himself promises to fight for his people against their enemies.

How many times we have failed because we believed that the battle was ours to fight. Instead of running to our "big brother," we stood up against the foe in our own strength only to realize that he was far stronger than we were, and we were sent running, battered and bruised. Many have trusted in their spirituality and have failed. You can be a new believer and have no real experience with the Lord at all and be strong in his strength. The one who is strong in the Lord is the person in need who runs to the Lord to ask him to handle a situation. The Psalmist put it this way in Psalm 60:12: "With God we will gain the victory, and he will trample down our enemies." With God as our big brother, there is nothing that can defeat us. We can do all things through Christ who strengthens us (see Philippians 4:13).

Be Strong in His Mighty Power

There is just one final thing we need to see in this verse. Paul told the Ephesians that the strength that was at their disposal was a "mighty power." Imagine if all the brilliant minds, armies, weapons, and artillery of the nations were at our disposal. That would be incredible power. Consider for a moment, however, that the God of heaven laughs at such shows of strength. One simple breath from his lips and the massive armies of this world are reduced to nothing. We have at our disposal a power that is far greater than anything this world has ever known. One simple word from the mouth of Jesus sends the demons of hell into disarray. They are powerless before him.

Why be content with your limited resources when the power of God Almighty is at your disposal? When the enemy presses in against you, run to Jesus. When temptations seem to overwhelm you, run to Jesus. When you feel the attack of Satan and his angels, run to Jesus. You cannot overcome these obstacles by yourself, but Jesus can. Be strong in his strength, not yours. Keep running to him. Nothing can stand against his mighty power.

For Consideration:

- Who or what are you depending on for victory in your Christian life? Do you trust in your experience and knowledge of Jesus or do you trust the living Jesus himself?

- How can you strengthen yourself in the Lord each day?

- What keeps you from experiencing Christ's strength in your life?

- What particular problem are you facing today? Can the Lord give you strength and wisdom to handle that problem?

For Prayer:

- Do you need God's strength to overcome a particular issue in your life? Run to Jesus and ask him to deal with this issue.

- Thank the Lord that he has placed his mighty power at your disposal.

- Ask him to show you when you are not trusting in him. Ask him to give you the courage and humility necessary to wait on him and trust in his leading and strength instead of your own.

25

Put On the Armor

Read Ephesians 6:11, 13

A s believers, we are involved in a spiritual warfare. In the last meditation, Paul challenged the Ephesians, in light of the battle that raged around them, to be made "strong in the Lord." He told them next that they were also to put on the whole armor of God. Let's consider what Paul had to say about this armor in verse 11 and verse 13.

The Full Armor of God

What soldier would go to war without wearing his protective clothing? All too many believers do not understand the need for armor. They feel that because they are believers, they are sheltered from the enemy's arrows. "I'm trusting in the Lord," they say. "I don't need to worry." These believers go about their daily routine feeling that there is nothing that can harm them. What we need to understand is that we are Satan's targets because we are the children of God. Everyone knows that the enemy does not fight his own men. Being a believer guarantees that we will be in the enemy's sights. It is for this reason that we need to be protected.

Notice that the armor we are to wear is defensive in nature. In other words, the armor is not so much for fighting as for protecting. The belt, the breastplate, the shoes, the shield, the helmet, and even the sword are all defensive in nature. Notice that God does not tell us to arm ourselves with spears, slingshots, and bows and arrows. Why does he tell us to clothe ourselves with protective armor? Should he not rather encourage us to take up our offensive weapons and do battle? In the last meditation, we discovered that the battle belongs to the Lord. We do not have the strength in ourselves to defeat the enemy. God does not give us offensive weapons because he wants to fight this battle for us.

God knows the tactics of the enemy better than we do. He has determined for us the best type of protection possible. The armor that God gives us, if worn, will protect us from any attack of the enemy. The secret, however, is to put this armor on daily. Without it we are vulnerable. You might ask, "Why do we need armor if God is there to protect us?" The answer, quite simply, is that this is God's means of protecting us. If we refuse to wear the armor and fall prey to one of Satan's arrows, the fault lies squarely on our own shoulders. While God is committed to doing the fighting for us, he has decided to protect us by giving us a full suit of armor.

Notice here that Paul tells us that we are to put on the "whole" armor of God. What good is a partial suit of armor? What if a soldier put on his shield and shoes but not his helmet? This would provide an open target for the enemy. The thing about the armor of God is that we must put on the whole suit of armor. To put on everything but one piece is to lose the battle. Satan is an excellent marksman. You can be sure that if there is a missing piece of armor, his arrow will find its way to that particular area. This is why Paul tells us to put on the "whole" armor. Every piece must be worn if the armor is to be effective. Let's now look at the reason for this armor.

Taking Your Stand

The first reason for wearing the armor, according to Paul,

is so that we might be able to stand. We are the targets of the enemy's arrows. He will not let up in his attack against us. His goal is to cause us to fall. The armor of God alone will give us the ability to stand. Wearing this armor, we can penetrate the enemy lines. Satan's flaming arrows will not cause us to fall.

The battle against evil is long and hard. You may say, "I'm a believer, how can I fall?" The believer can fall prey to all the temptations of the unbeliever. Immorality, greed, lust, and pride are all possible in the life of the believer. We have all seen Christians whose commitment to the Lord Jesus has become so eroded that they are no longer distinguishable from unbelievers. Many Christians believe that they are magically protected from Satan's attacks because they are believers. Throughout the Scriptures are stories of godly men and women who fell because they were unguarded at a moment in time. Without this armor we will fall also.

The Devil's Schemes

The second reason why we need to put on the whole armor of God is because of the devil's evil schemes. The enemy is very cunning and sly. He is the master of deceit and trickery. The Greek word for "scheme" comes from two words literally meaning "to travel with." Satan is watching our every move. He will "travel with" us to spy out our weaknesses or to whisper lies into our ears. He has us in his sight. All it takes is for us to let down our guards for a moment, and we will be pierced through by one of his arrows.

I remember going out for a morning coffee with my wife, Diane. As we traveled the thought came to me that Diane often got cold. Somehow I began to resent this. It was as if Satan were saying to me, "Wayne, just think of all the things you and Diane could do if she didn't use the excuse of it being too cold." I felt Satan whisper in my ear, "If she really loved you, she wouldn't be thinking so much about her own comfort."

We arrived at the coffee shop, sat down, and began to engage in conversation. Some time into this conversation, the waitress walked over to the air conditioner and turned it on. That cold air seemed to be directed right at us. In just a few minutes, Diane looked at me and said, "I'm cold; could we leave?" We did leave and went to a nearby store. The first words that came out of her mouth when we entered the air-conditioned store were, "It's cold in here."

Needless to say, I got quite frustrated with her. Satan had been using this issue to get between us all morning. He had been planting thoughts in my mind that would cause me to get angry and frustrated. I thank God that he gave me enough discernment that day to recognize this as an attack of the enemy. I was able to recognize this attack and resist it. The incident, however, showed me how subtle the schemes of the enemy really are. He had been "traveling with me," seeking an appropriate moment to cause me to fall. I can't tell you how often I have fallen into other such traps.

I have seen Satan's work in prayer meetings. I've been part of Bible studies where Satan caused someone to become very passionate about a particular issue. While their passion was wonderful, it was misplaced and began to heat up the discussion and eventually led to serious division among God's people. Satan is a schemer. He will not hesitate to come right into our prayer meetings or studies. He will rile up hearts and attitudes. He will do everything he can to cause division and trouble among believers.

You can never tell when the enemy will strike you. It may be in a moment of great victory when his arrow of pride pierces. It may be in a moment of tremendous defeat when he causes discouragement to overwhelm. Maybe it will be when you are alone with no one to whom you are accountable. It could be in a crowd of people that he shoots his arrows of bitterness and envy. It may even be when you are quietly enjoying a coffee with the one you love. Satan is always scheming. You can never afford to be without your armor.

The Day of Evil

The final reason given here in these verses for wearing the armor of God is because of the day of evil that is coming. To what day does this refer? The Bible teaches us that as the day of the Lord approaches, there will be an increase in wickedness and sin on the earth. Mark 13 tells us that in the last days, we will see an increase of wars, famine, and earthquakes. Believers will be delivered up to be judged. We will be hated for Christ's sake. In 2 Timothy 3:12 we are reminded that we will suffer because of Christ. The book of Revelation paints a picture of persecution in the last days. What we are presently going through is nothing compared to what we can expect in the final days before the return of our Lord. When Satan is unleashed he will bring with him tremendous persecution on the church.

Since the fall of mankind, every day has been full of the evil of sin and death. History has already recounted for us the story of countless believers who have been tortured for their faith. The Bible teaches us that there is a day coming when these stories of persecution will increase. What will keep us through the evil days now and those that are to come? God has given us his armor to keep us from falling. Only those who wear this armor will stand in evil days.

For Consideration:

• What do these verses teach us about our enemy Satan?

• Why is it important that we put on the full armor of God?

• Have you ever been pierced by one of Satan's arrows? How could the armor of God have protected you on that occasion?

• Why do you suppose we have heard so little teaching on the subject of spiritual warfare in our day? Is there any relation between this lack of teaching and the present state of the church?

For Prayer:

• Ask God to help you to put on this armor.

- Thank the Lord that he does not leave us defenseless before the enemy. Ask him to show you if there are pieces that you have not yet put on.

- Ask God to open your eyes to the real nature of the battle that surrounds you today.

26

Spiritual Forces of Evil

Read Ephesians 6:12

So far in this section of Scripture, we have seen that we need two things in our battle against the forces of evil. Verse 10 reminds us that we need strength. This strength is not our own but the Lord's. Second, we need protection. Verses 11 and 13 tell us to put on the armor of God so that we can stand in the day of battle. The third thing we need for the battle is knowledge of our enemy. Paul spoke about this in verse 12.

I always remember the story of a missionary who went to a certain town to hold a missionary meeting only to find that he had forgotten which church in that town had invited him to do the meeting. He knew what he was supposed to do but did not know where he was to do it. There are many Christians today who know that they are to be fighting a battle but do not know where the battle is. This is just where Satan wants us. It brings him great delight to have us fight the wrong battle.

There are churches all around us who are fighting to maintain their denominational distinctions, their traditions, or their unique understandings of the Word of God. Some of these same churches have failed to produce believers who are in love with the Lord Jesus and producing spiritual fruit in their lives. Instead, they are constantly at each other's throats, trying to prove that their way is closer to the truth. Such battles are the delight of Satan. He has succeeded in blinding our eyes to the nature of the battle. As long as we are fighting the wrong battle, he has no reason for concern.

If there is one thing that Paul wants us to understand in this verse, it is the nature of the battle. "Our struggle," wrote Paul, "is not against flesh and blood." By "flesh and blood" Paul was referring to human beings. Because the real battle is not in the physical realm, it cannot be fought by means of physical weapons. If this is the case, our Bible schools and seminaries need to be teaching more about spiritual warfare. We need to see pastors and missionaries who are able to deal with spiritual problems by doing spiritual warfare. We need to see church leaders who recognize a spiritual attack and know what to do about it. All too often we are like those who try to get rid of the weeds in their gardens by cutting off the individual stalks instead of pulling up the roots. Could it be that the reason for the defeat we experience is because we are trying to fight spiritual enemies with physical weapons? Let's look at what Paul wrote about our enemy in this verse.

Rulers, Authorities, and Powers of This Dark World

Paul tells us in this verse that our battle is against rulers, authorities, and powers of this dark world. Who or what are these rulers, authorities, and powers? At first glance it might appear that they represent political or religious leaders of our day. This, however, would be contrary to what Paul is telling us in the first part of this verse. He just told us that our battle was not against flesh and blood. So he cannot be referring to the human leaders of this world.

In John 12:31 and John 14:30, Jesus spoke of Satan as being the "prince of this world." In 2 Corinthians 4:4 Paul referred to Satan as the "god of this age." The apostle John reminded his readers in 1 John 5:19 that the whole world is under the control of the "evil one." The kingdom over which Satan rules is described as being a dark kingdom of orgies, drunkenness, sexual immorality, debauchery, dissension, and jealousy (Romans 13:12–13). Believers have been rescued from this dominion of darkness and placed in the kingdom of light (Colossians 1:12–13). Having said this, who then are the rulers, authorities, and powers of this dark world? While Satan may use human beings in positions of leadership, he himself is said to be the "prince of this world" and the "god of this age." He and his angels are the rulers of this present darkness.

While Satan and his host of angels are currently ruling over this world, they have already been defeated by the death of Christ on the cross. Speaking of Jesus, Paul stated in Colossians 2:15: "And having disarmed the powers and authorities, he made a public spectacle of them, triumphing over them by the cross." And again in 1 Corinthians 15:24 Paul stated: "Then the end will come, when he hands over the kingdom to God the Father after he has destroyed all dominion, authority and power."

It is against these spiritual forces of Satan that we are daily wrestling. We cannot underestimate their influence in government, education, and our everyday life. They use our natural tendency to sin to their advantage. Satan would like to keep us blind to his presence in our society and private lives. If he can cause us to think that evil spirits and demons are figments of our imagination, he has won half the battle. Satan and his angels are very real. They move throughout this world, seeking to advance their dark kingdom. They are the source of many of the problems and evil we see in our society. Our fight is against them. No wonder Paul tells us to be "strong in the Lord" and to put on our spiritual armor.

Spiritual Forces of Evil in the Heavenly Realms
    Notice second that Paul told the Ephesians that their enemy could not be seen. These invisible wicked forces live in the "heavenly realms." There is more to reality than the physical

things we see around us. There is an unseen spiritual realm where holy angels and fallen angels are engaged in spiritual warfare.

How do we fight an enemy we cannot see? If we are to fight this battle, we will first need to clothe ourselves with the spiritual armor God has given us to wear. Second, we will also need to cling tightly to the Word of God, which is our only authoritative guide to God's perfect will. Finally, we will need to be strong in the Lord. Part of what it means to be strong in the Lord is to accept the spiritual gifts and authority he has given us to wage this battle in his name in the heavenly realms. If we seek the Lord, he will give us the wisdom and discernment necessary to recognize and be wise to the schemes of this enemy. Only clothed in his armor and depending on his strength alone, we can overcome the rulers of the dark kingdom.

For Consideration:

- How much are we aware of the spiritual battle around us today?

- How does a good understanding of the nature of the battle change how we fight that battle?

- To what extent do we realize the true nature of the battle we face in our world today?

For Prayer:

- Ask God to open your eyes to the true nature of the battle before you today.

- Thank the Lord that he gives you the tools necessary to fight this battle.

- Ask the Lord to clothe you with his strength and the armor he provides so that you will be protected.

27

The Belt of Truth

Read Ephesians 6:14

P aul began his description of the various pieces of armor with the belt of truth. It should be understood here that the order of these pieces is not an indication of their priority. Every piece of armor is vital to the soldier. Some commentators see the order Paul used here simply as being the order in which a soldier would normally put on his armor. Let's consider now this first piece of armor.

The truth spoken of here is twofold. The word in the original language can refer to sincerity of character. Have you ever listened to someone talk about an issue when you knew that they did not practice what they preached? We rarely take seriously what these people say. Do you suppose that the spiritual forces in heavenly realms will take us seriously when we seek to do battle with them without sincerity before God? The spiritual battle is not for the hypocrite.

If you are not right with the Lord, then the very first thing you need to do is to confess your sin and be reconciled to him. Jesus tells us that if our brother has something against us, we are to leave our gift at the altar and be reconciled with our brother before offering our gift (Matthew 5:23–24). If in worship we need to be reconciled with God, would this not also be true in our wrestling with the powers of this dark world? Victory in this spiritual battle before us begins with a right relationship with God. We need to confess our sins. We need to go to those we have offended and be reconciled. We need to deal with the secret thoughts and attitudes of the heart. As long as these things remain unresolved, we give the enemy a foothold in our lives. How can we expect to defeat the enemy when we continue to allow him access into our lives through these sins? If you want to do battle with the enemy you must sincerely love the Lord Jesus. You must love him enough to close the door to sin in any form. This is the first aspect of the belt of truth.

Truth is not only related to our character but also to our understanding of reality. If there is one thing the enemy excels in, it is falsehood and lies. Jesus said in John 8:44 to the religious leaders of his day: "You belong to your father, the devil, and you want to carry out your father's desire. He was a murderer from the beginning, not holding to the truth, for there is no truth in him. When he lies, he speaks his native language, for he is a liar and the father of lies."

Jesus tells us very plainly here that there is no truth in the devil. He is the father of lies. Back in the garden of Eden, Satan lied to Eve by telling her that she would not die if she ate from the forbidden tree. She ate from the tree, and this led to spiritual death. Our enemy has continued to lie. Why should he change his tactic when it seems to work so well for him?

The lies of Satan are of various sorts. He lies to us first about the person of God and his Word. This was the nature of his attack of Eve in the garden of Eden. He lied to her and caused her to wonder if God's Word was really true. Do you wonder why so many seminaries and Bible schools have been questioning the authority of the Bible? It really should not surprise us to find evidence of the enemy's attack. He knows that if he can cause us to cast aside the truth of God, he has an open door to do as he pleases in our society. Without the moral standards of the Bible to hinder him, he is free to lead people into all kinds of immorality and perversion. Without the clear teaching of Scripture, he can have people think what they want about God. We will speak of the place of the Word of God in greater detail later. Suffice it to say that Satan excels in trying to pervert our thoughts about God and his Word.

Another area that Satan seeks to attack is in the area of who we are in Christ. He delights in distorting the truth of our security as believers. He may tempt us to believe that God could never accept us because of our sin. He may cause us to think that we are failures. He may create situations that would lead us to believe that God has abandoned us. Where do we turn in these situations? God's word, as contained in the pages of Holy Scripture, is our only real source of truth. We must cling to this truth in our times of spiritual attack. There are times when the truth alone is all we need to be set free from the lies of the enemy. "Then you will know the truth, and the truth will set you free" (John 8:32).

There have been times in my life when I have believed the lies of Satan. I have often wondered how God could accept me. I have often felt like I was an utter failure. Doubts have plagued my mind and left me discouraged and despairing. Victory came for me in these situations only when I realized that I was listening to the lies of Satan. I had to reject them in favor of the inspired Word of God. Only the truth could set me free. When I claimed the truth of God, Satan was forced to let me go.

The apostle James tells us in James 4:7 that we are to resist the devil and he will flee from us. How do we resist the devil? We resist him in the area of truth. We resist his lies and his falsehood and turn from them to the truth of the Word of God. Satan will have no recourse but to flee and to leave us alone. The sooner we realize that our battle is with the "father of lies," the sooner we will understand the importance of wearing the belt of truth. When Satan's lies bind us, only the truth of God can give us victory.

Why is truth so important in the spiritual warfare before us? We have said that the truth spoken of here has to do, first, with our character and, secondly, with our understanding of reality. Let's break these down and examine them more fully.

It is important that we experience integrity of character for two reasons. First, insincerity will destroy our witness for the Lord. Isn't this exactly what the enemy wants to do? If we are not right with God, then our witness will be hindered. People will see us as we really are. They will see our attitudes and our actions. They will hear those things we say. If we are living in sin, we cannot be a good witness for the Lord. Many people turn their backs on the Lord because of the hypocrisy they see in his servants. Honor is vital if we are to be lights in this dark world.

Second, lack of sincerity will make us powerless before the foe. Would you send a sick soldier to battle if you didn't have to? In a similar way, our sin and hypocrisy weaken us in the battle. Remember the story of how one man stole some goods from the city of Jericho after God clearly told the Israelites they were to take nothing (Joshua 7)? When the children of Israel then marched against the little town of Ai, they were defeated. Joshua asked the Lord why they suffered defeat at Ai following such a great victory over the larger city of Jericho. The Lord told him it was because of the sin in their midst. The church cannot expect to be victorious over the spiritual forces of this dark world if its members are living in sin. While God may be gracious to us even in our sin, true victory only comes through living in obedience to the Lord Jesus.

Satan's lies can discourage us in the battle. How many times have we lost our courage because we believed the lie of Satan that God had abandoned us? How many times have we failed in prayer because we believed some lie Satan was whispering in our ears? How often have true servants of God been discouraged by the demonic deception that they were not accomplishing anything, and it would be better for them to pack their bags and go home? There are so many variations on these lies that we cannot even begin to touch on all the ways that Satan can discourage God's servants. Only the truth in the Word of God can give us the strength to go on.

Let me conclude here with a final statement about how this belt of truth helps us in our battle against our spiritual enemies. We understand that Satan's kingdom is built on lies. Just as it takes light to conquer darkness, so it takes truth to conquer the lies of Satan. In order for Satan to build his kingdom, he has to deceive people into believing his lies. The only remedy for this is belief in the truth of the Bible. Only the truth of God can set us free from the errors of Satan. In order to be victorious over Satan, we must recognize these attacks of the enemy and resist them with the truth.

There will be times when you hear Satan telling you that it is all right to sin, because nobody will know. You may feel him trying to tell you that it is only natural that you feel the way you do and that you should not be ashamed to let yourself go. What do you do when Satan attacks you with his arrow of falsehood and lies? Step one is to recognize this falsehood as being from the enemy. Step two is to resist it as a lie. Step three is to counter it with God's truth in God's Word. We will have more to say about how we recognize falsehood at a later point. When you are being tempted, ask yourself, "What is the truth in this matter?" Ask God to make the truth clear, and then wrap it around you like a belt, and set out to resist the lies of the enemy in Jesus' name.

For Consideration:

• What two aspects of truth are discussed here in this meditation?

• Scripture teaches us that Satan is the father of lies. How has he been using these lies in our day?

• How do we counter the lies of Satan?

• Are there any lies that you have believed?

- Why is sincerity of character an important aspect of truth? How does this help us to do battle with the enemy?

For Prayer:

- Ask God to make the lies of Satan clear to you. Ask him to reveal any ways in which you are deceived.

- Ask God to examine you to be sure that you have a sincere character.

- Ask God to reveal his truth to your community. Ask him to set your community free from the lies of the enemy.

28

The Breastplate of Righteousness

Read Ephesians 6:14

The second piece of armor the believer is to put on, according to Paul, is the breastplate of righteousness. This breastplate covered the soldier from his neck down to his thighs. It protected all his vital organs. Paul told the Ephesians that the breastplate is "righteousness." What is this righteousness and how is it to be used in the spiritual battle before us?

The Greek word used here is *"dikaiosune."* This word can be translated as "innocent," "faultless," or "guiltless." It is used of those who are in a right relationship with God. There are many opinions about what it means to be right with God.

In the New Testament we meet a group of people called the Pharisees, who were very religious. They prided themselves in the strictest observation of the law of Moses. In the eyes of the Jewish community, Pharisees were the most righteous people. Speaking about the Pharisees in Matthew 5:20, Jesus said: "For I tell you that unless your righteousness surpasses that of the Pharisees and the teachers of the law, you will certainly not enter the kingdom of heaven."

This is a very important verse. Jesus is telling us here that our righteousness needs to surpass that of these Pharisees. Their righteousness was self-righteousness, consisting of external obedience to the law. Jesus is telling us that we need a righteousness that goes beyond outward obedience to the law of God. Legalism is not the same as true righteousness. You can be a careful observer of God's law. You can separate yourself from ungodly things in your life. You can *do* all the right things and still not *be* in a right relationship with God. Righteousness goes far deeper than outward actions. A closer examination of the Pharisees reveals that they were a very proud people. They loved to have people praise them because of their apparent holiness and devout lives. While they observed all the right laws, their hearts were far from God (Matthew 15:7–9).

When Samuel went out to anoint a king over Israel, the Lord led him to the household of Jesse. Samuel fell into the trap of looking at the physical strength and appearance of each of Jesse's sons who came before him. God reminded him that he did not see things as humans saw them. In 1 Samuel 16:7 we read: "But the LORD said to Samuel, 'Do not consider his appearance or his height, for I have rejected him. The LORD does not look at the things man looks at. Man looks at the outward appearance, but the LORD looks at the heart.'"

We all know that it is important to live according to the standards laid out for us in the Scriptures. We should not assume, however, that just because we do all the right things, we are in a right relationship with God. We can be sitting in church every week with our children quietly sitting beside us and not be righteous. We can give our tithes and offerings on a regular basis and be as far away from the Lord as the person who doesn't know him at all. Our righteousness is not based on how much we obey the letter of God's law. There are many who mistake the breastplate of legalism for the breastplate of righteousness. In the battle before us, we cannot afford to make this mistake. God is looking for a righteousness that goes far deeper than heartless obedience to rules.

Very closely connected to the breastplate of legalism is the breastplate of good works. There are those who believe that to be righteous we need to love God and our neighbor and do good to those around us. While all of these things are admirable, they are not to be equated with the breastplate of righteousness. We have all met unbelievers who live good and moral lives. Can those who have never accepted the work of Christ be said to be righteous simply because they live a good life?

There is also the breastplate of good theology. Some feel that they are righteous because they believe the Bible and have good doctrine. Even Satan believes a lot of truth. He believes that Jesus is the Son of God, but Satan is certainly not righteous.

What I am trying to say here is that you can have the proper lifestyle, do many good deeds, follow the traditions of your spiritual fathers, and believe all the right things about Jesus and still not be clothed with the breastplate of righteousness. If righteousness is not all these things, what is it?

The righteousness that Paul wrote about here is a right standing before God that is given to us by faith. Paul tells us in Romans 3:21–22: "But now a righteousness from God, apart from law, has been made known, to which the Law and the Prophets testify. This righteousness from God comes through faith in Jesus Christ to all who believe. There is no difference."

If there was anyone who could have boasted about his faithful service to the Lord Jesus, it was the apostle Paul. He was beaten more times for his Lord than all the other apostles. He had been a Pharisee who observed the law of God with exact precision. He had all the right training. His zeal for the Lord was unmatched in his day. Listen to what this great missionary said concerning his great achievements and credentials in Philippians 3:8–9: "What is more, I consider everything a loss compared to the surpassing greatness of knowing Christ Jesus my Lord, for whose sake I have lost all things. I consider them rubbish, that I may gain Christ and be found in him, not having a righteousness of my own that comes from the law, but that which is through faith in Christ—the righteousness that comes from God and is by faith."

Notice that Paul was not interested in having a righteousness of his own. He was looking for the righteousness that comes by faith in Christ Jesus. This is the righteousness that he spoke about here in this verse. This righteousness is a right standing with God that is given to believers as a gift through faith. It is undeserved and unmerited. It cannot be earned. None of us is worthy of it. All of us are guilty sinners who deserve divine judgment. God, however, is willing to pardon, forgive our offenses, and wipe our slates clean. He does this through the death and resurrection of his Son Jesus. Jesus came to offer absolute pardon and forgiveness. There is no way to earn this righteousness. It is given only to those who trust in the work of the Lord Jesus on their behalf. Listen to what Paul told the Romans in Romans 4:4–5: "Now when a man works, his wages are not credited to him as a gift, but as an obligation. However, to the man who does not work but trusts God who justifies the wicked, his faith is credited as righteousness."

You are not righteous because of what you do but because of what the Lord Jesus does for you. This breastplate has nothing to do with all the good things you do for the Lord Jesus. Satan cares nothing for those good works. Your external obedience will not protect you. What good is it to say to Satan, "You can't touch me; look at all the good things I've done for the Lord." Do you think Satan will stop attacking you simply because you have done all kinds of good things for the Lord in the past? Be assured that your past record of obedience will only encourage him to attack you further.

How does the righteousness that Christ gives us as a gift help us in the battle against the enemy? First, if we are trusting in the righteousness that the Lord himself provides, the enemy cannot discourage us. We know that our relationship with Christ is not based on our achievements and successes but rather on the finished work of Christ on the cross for us. When Satan tells us that we are miserable sinners, we can respond, "Yes, I am a sinner, but Christ died for me and despite my shortcomings I am still his child." When Satan asks us if we are sure we have done enough good deeds to be accepted by God, we simply say, "Satan, the only deed that matters is the death of my Lord on the cross." He has no alternative then but to retreat, a defeated foe because of the righteousness of Christ dwelling in us.

Second, when we depend on Christ's righteousness, we send Satan straight to Christ to do battle. If we are trusting in our own good works to get to heaven, we can be sure that Satan will give us real cause to wonder if we have done enough. All of us have fallen short. If, however, we are depending on the righteousness of Christ and his death on the cross for us, Satan must do battle with Christ himself because we are placing our full confidence in his work. Satan cannot defeat Christ and his work. Satan knows that he was defeated at the cross. Again, he must retreat.

Paul challenged the Ephesians to put on the breastplate of the righteousness of the Lord Jesus that covers all those who realize that they cannot defeat the foe through their own good works and efforts. How do we put on this breastplate of righteousness? First, we recognize that our own efforts are not sufficient. Second, we accept that the only righteousness that God requires is the righteousness of his Son Jesus. Third, we trust Jesus to cover us in his righteousness and call out in faith to him to clothe us. Only in his goodness and righteousness can we be protected. Satan can not stand against the perfect work of Christ for us and in us.

For Consideration:

- What are the various ways people try to be righteous in our day? Why do all of these methods fall short of God's standard?

- Have you been clothed in the righteousness of Christ? How do you know?

- What does the righteousness of Christ do for us that our own righteousness could never do?

- How does trusting in Christ's righteousness in us protect us from the enemy and his attacks?

For Prayer:

- Do you know people who are trusting in their own righteousness to save them? Take a moment to pray for them.

- Thank the Lord for his righteousness applied to our lives and the assurance this gives us of victory over Satan.

29

The Sandals of the Gospel

Read Ephesians 6:15

What armor would be complete without footwear? Can you imagine a soldier dressed up with all his armor going into battle barefoot? The Roman sandals were a vital part of a Roman soldier's equipment. Our sandals, according to Paul, are the "preparation of the gospel" (NKJV) or the "readiness that comes from the gospel of peace" (NIV). What did Paul mean here?

Some would place the emphasis on our readiness to share the message of the gospel with others. There can be no question that we need to be a people who are always ready to share the message of the gospel with others. Paul himself was a very powerful example of this. He was willing to lay down his life for the sake of the gospel. Peter too challenges us to be always ready to share with others the reason for the hope that is in us: "But in your hearts set apart Christ as Lord. Always be prepared to give an answer to everyone who asks you to give the reason for the hope that you have. But do this with gentleness and respect" (1 Peter 3:15).

It is by means of the gospel that the sinner is set free from the power of the enemy and brought into the family of God. The question, however, is whether this is what Paul meant by the sandals of "readiness that comes from the gospel." Is Paul telling us that if we want to be able to stand against the powerful spiritual forces of darkness we need to be out on the streets witnessing for Jesus? Is this our protection from the enemy? I believe that there is a far deeper significance to this verse.

We have already seen that it is not our righteousness that is going to keep us from falling prey to the attacks of the enemy. It is a good thing to share the gospel with those who need the Lord, but this will not keep us from falling prey to the attacks of the enemy. Even those who are faithful witnesses for the Lord fall into sin.

The key to understanding this piece of equipment is our understanding of the word "readiness." What this verse seems to say is that the gospel itself is our preparation. Our readiness to face the spiritual forces around us is found in the gospel. It is not our readiness to *share* the gospel that is in focus here but rather our *experience of* the gospel. We are not protected by our personal efforts to bring the gospel to others. Our protection comes from the application of the gospel to our own lives.

What is this gospel that Paul spoke about in this passage? The gospel, according to Paul in Romans 1:16, is the "power of God for the salvation of everyone who believes" (NKJV). Notice that Paul said that the gospel is a power. This gospel is far more than words or thoughts; it is power. Isn't this what we need in our battle against the enemy? We need power to face this spiritual adversary. That power can be found in the gospel. Paul repeated this thought in 1 Thessalonians 1:5 when he said: "Our gospel came to you not simply with words, but also with power, with the Holy Spirit and with deep conviction."

What is this power of the gospel that Paul spoke about here? This power can be seen, first, in its ability to rescue the sinner from the hands of Satan. We cannot underestimate the power of Satan. His deceit and cunning are beyond our natural ability to resist. There is only one thing that can rescue us from Satan's deceit in combination with our own natural tendency to sin—the gospel alone. This gospel has the power to free those trapped in the bondage of sin. No amount of personal struggle against the enemy could ever have rescued us from the tremendous grip of Satan on our lives. Can you remember the day you not only heard the message of the gospel but also experienced its power? On that day your chains fell off. Your blind eyes were opened, and you saw for the first time that you were indeed a prisoner of Satan. The enemy had no power against this gospel. His grip was loosened, and you were set free by the greater power of the gospel.

Not only does this gospel have power to free us from the grip of Satan, it also has power to forgive and heal our sin. Those who have experienced the power of the gospel can testify to its cleansing power. The gospel is far more than words on a paper. It is far more than good news of a Savior. It is a power that cleanses and forgives. You may have been the worst sinner on earth. The power of the gospel can wipe every one of your sins clean. Nothing you ever did will be held against you because the gospel has the power to forgive your past. Not only this, the gospel also has the power to heal you of your sin. Those sins that once held you captive will hold you no longer. The gospel will renew your character. You will never be the same again. As Paul said in 2 Corinthians 5:17: "Therefore, if anyone is in Christ, he is a new creation; the old has gone, the new has come!"

The power of the gospel is seen in its ability to take hardened sinners and transform their character through the forgiveness of sin. This same gospel will send the hosts of hell into retreat. They have been defeated by this gospel. They know that they cannot stand against its power. They are helpless before it. Paul wrote in Romans 8:37–39 that nothing can separate us from the love of God, not even hell itself: "No, in all these things we are more than conquerors through him who loved us. For I am convinced that neither death nor life, *neither angels nor demons*, neither the present nor the future, nor any powers, neither height nor depth, nor anything else in all creation, will be able to separate us from the love of God that is in Christ Jesus our Lord."

This is the power of the gospel. The gospel is not just words about a Savior. It is a power without equal in this universe. It is the power of forgiveness and pardon. It is the power of life and death. It is our stable foundation and defense against the arrows of the enemy.

Fitting our feet with the readiness that comes from the gospel has to do with experiencing the power of the gospel in our lives. It is one thing to know the words of the gospel, and it is another to experience its power. The Roman army's sandals of Paul's day had nails in them for gripping the ground in combat. Similarly, our protection here against the forces of evil is nothing less than the confidence to stand firm on solid ground, knowing that we are at peace with God through the gospel of Christ.

Has your experience of the gospel gone beyond words? Has your life been transformed by this gospel? Have you experienced the freedom it offers? When the enemy approaches you, is he pushed back by the power of this life-transforming gospel evidenced in your life?

Only those who have put on the sandals of the gospel are able to stand firm and resist the enemy. Only the power of what Christ has done for us in this gospel can protect us from the onslaught of the enemy. If we want to be protected in this great spiritual battle that rages on around us, we need to experience the wonderful salvation of God that is recorded for us in the gospel. If you have not experienced the full power of this gospel, you need to cry out to Jesus right now. Ask God to apply the power of the gospel to your life to heal and forgive you of your sins. Only the gospel can set you free. If you want to be prepared for the battle before you, you need to have the sandals of the gospel strapped securely to your feet.

For Consideration:

- What does Paul mean when he told the Ephesians that they needed to put on the sandals of the gospel?

- How has the gospel transformed your life? Do you see continued evidence of the transforming power of the gospel in your life? Give examples.

- What is the place of the gospel in the spiritual battle that rages around us? How does the gospel protect us from Satan and his attacks?

For Prayer:

- Thank God for the way he demonstrated the power of the gospel in your life. Thank him for the changes the gospel has made in your life.

- Thank the Lord that you can have confidence in the battle against the enemy now that you have accepted the message of the gospel.

- Take a moment to pray that God would reveal the power of the gospel to an unbelieving friend or relative.

30

The Shield of Faith

Read Ephesians 6:16

The next piece of armor Paul spoke about was the shield. Commentators tell us that there were two types of shields used in Paul's day. The first was a round shield measuring approximately 3 feet (or about 90 centimeters) in diameter. The second type of shield was more rectangular in shape. It measured just over 2 1/2 feet wide (about 80 centimeters) and almost 4 feet high (1.2 meters). Paul spoke here in this passage about this second shield, which protected much more of the soldier than the first. As you can imagine, a shield this size would have been a greater hindrance to fighting the battle than the smaller one. We need to remember, however, that our battle really belongs to the Lord and that these pieces of armor are more for defense. Our part in the battle with Satan is mostly to resist him. This shield is a vital part of that resistance.

Paul told the Ephesians that this shield is the shield of faith. It was by means of this shield of faith that the Ephesians could extinguish the "flaming arrows of the evil one." In the days of Paul, soldiers would dip their arrows in a tar-like substance and set them on fire before shooting them from their bows. This multiplied the damage caused by the arrows. Not only would victims have to deal with flesh wounds, but whatever the arrows struck might also be set on fire. To combat these flaming arrows, the wooden shields were covered in leather to retard the flames before they could catch the wood on fire.

The first thing we need to understand from this verse is that the enemy is shooting his flaming arrows at us continuously. Notice that Paul did not say that we should carry the shield of faith just in case the enemy should shoot his arrow at us. The assumption here is that this is going to happen. Every day of our lives, we are being bombarded with these flaming arrows. There are a number of flaming arrows the enemy may send our way. Let's consider a few of them.

Doubt and Discouragement

Have you ever been subject to doubt and discouragement? I remember feeling this way after a special evangelistic event I had participated in. I did not doubt my salvation; I was sure of that. What I did doubt, however, was the spiritual gifts the Lord had given me for service. I began to lament the fact that I was not as close to the Lord as I would like. I wondered where God was and why he was not more real to me. After Elijah's great triumph on Mount Carmel over the prophets of Baal, he too fell into a period of great discouragement and doubt (1 Kings 19). He wanted to die.

The strange thing about spiritual discouragement is that it often comes in times of victory. Where does this come from? Is this not one of Satan's flaming arrows sent to sidetrack us and keep us from advancing the kingdom?

How do we overcome these attacks? Only an absolute confidence in the Word of God that tells us that we are secure in him will give us victory over such an attack. Sometimes everything around us seems to be falling apart. Our emotions betray us, and we don't feel like a child of God. In those times only our faith and confidence in God will take us through. When the flaming arrow of discouragement strikes our shield of faith, it is immediately extinguished because we trust in him who cannot fail.

Sinful Desires

What about those flaming arrows of sinful desires and attitudes? Lust and greed are examples of these arrows. These weapons of fire will quickly ignite and consume our whole being if not quickly extinguished. Who among us has never encountered these stinging arrows? In our natural strength, we would surely fall.

Sinful Attitudes

Another flaming arrow of Satan comes in the form of wrong attitudes toward others. When that arrow strikes, it does not take long before it ignites our whole being with bitterness, jealousy, and anger. Unless dealt with in Christ's name, it will quickly spread to other people and has been known to set whole churches ablaze with strife. We know how easily we could fall prey to these sinful attitudes. By faith we cry out to the Lord for strength to resist. In him alone there is victory. There are many other flaming arrows of Satan. I have given these, however, as examples of how the enemy continually attacks us.

What is faith and how does it help us overcome these flaming arrows? In Hebrews 11:1 we read that faith is "being sure of what we hope for and certain of what we do not see." Faith is "being sure" of what we do not see. It is an unseen confidence in the Lord and his purposes. Satan knows our limitations as human beings. He knows our natural blindness to the things of God and our inability to understand his ways. When Satan spoke with Eve in the garden of Eden, he tried to persuade her by very rational means that it was perfectly acceptable to eat of the tree of the knowledge of good and evil. He had a lot in his favor that day as he tempted Eve. He had the beauty of the tree itself. The fruit appeared to be very delicious. Even Eve's natural curiosity and desire for wisdom was working in Satan's favor (see Genesis 3:6). What would have kept her from falling in this moment of temptation?

Would it not have been her faith and confidence in what God had said?

Faith takes God at his word. There are times when evidence seems to point us in one way, but Scripture points us in another way. Faith will obey even when it cannot understand. It will willingly resist what appears to be logical and natural in favor of the Word of God. It will cast its full weight of confidence on God and his Word. When Satan says, "All evidence points to the fact that I am right," faith responds, "I still trust in what God says." When Satan says, "It's only natural to respond in this way," faith says, "God's Word tells me that I don't have to."

Faith not only takes God at his word but it also trusts God for the impossible. It recognizes that while things may appear to be out of reach, nothing is impossible for God. Faith will persevere when all odds are against it simply because it has an unshakeable confidence in God, who is able to do all things. When Satan seeks to discourage, faith responds, "All things are possible with God" (Mark 10:27).

Faith also attempts the impossible. It understands its limits and the human impossibility of the task before it but still perseveres in the strength of the Lord to win the victory. When Satan says, "You could never expect anyone to believe that," faith responds, "All good things are possible by God's grace." Faith is not held back by the obstacles strewn on the pathway. It jumps over the hurdles of discouragement and perseveres with confidence in the God of the impossible.

What can Satan do against faith? He is powerless before this confidence in the Lord. Satan's weapons of logical arguments will not work; attempts to discourage and distract will fail; lust and greed are quenched. The shield of faith extinguishes all these flaming arrows.

Where does faith come from? Ultimately, faith is a gift of God. You and I know that in our natural selves we do not have faith. In 1 Corinthians 12:9 we read that faith is a spiritual gift received through the Holy Spirit. As with any gift, this faith must be exercised if it is to grow into maturity in our lives. Paul wrote in Romans 10:17 that faith comes from hearing the word of God. James tells us that if we say we have faith but do not apply it to our lives, our faith is in vain (James 2:14–17). In other words, faith is matured in us as we listen to the Word of God and apply it to our lives.

What we need to understand here is that Satan is constantly shooting his flaming arrows at us. Sometimes it is our faith alone that will extinguish those flaming arrows. This faith is given to us as a gift of the Spirit of God, and it matures as we take God at his word.

Have you taken up this shield of faith? Ask God right now to clothe you in his gift of faith. This is a necessary part of the armor of the Christian. You cannot do without it. Expect God to answer this prayer as you respond in obedience to him and his Word. Hold tightly to this shield. Let nothing shake you from your confidence in God. He will not fail you if you rest in him and his Word.

For Consideration:

• What evidence have you seen in your life of these flaming arrows? Give some examples.

• What is faith?

• How does faith help us overcome the attacks of the enemy?

• Have you had times in your life when your faith enabled you to overcome the attack of the enemy? Give an example.

For Prayer:

• Ask God to increase your faith in him and his Word. Thank him that faith is a gift given to all who will receive and act on it.

- Ask God to help you recognize and resist the enemy's flaming arrows.

- Do you know someone who is being attacked by the flaming arrows of the enemy? Take a moment to pray for that person.

31

The Helmet of Salvation

Read Ephesians 6:17

We move now to the fifth piece of armor. Paul tells us to take the helmet of salvation. I do not believe that we need to read too much into these pieces of armor. Why should Paul speak of the helmet of salvation and not a breastplate of salvation or a belt of salvation? We are not told. What is important here is not where each piece of armor fits on the human body but what the pieces represent. There are several things we need to mention here about the helmet of salvation.

Paul tells us here to "take" the helmet of salvation. The word "take" is very important. The Greek word used here is translated over fifty times in the King James Version of the Bible by the word "receive." There are those who believe that they need to do something for this salvation. They believe that if they live a good life or believe the right things, then they will be given this helmet as a reward. They live their lives trying to be good enough to measure up to the standards that God has laid out in Scripture in the hope that their valiant efforts will be noticed by God, and they will be granted this wonderful salvation as a reward. Paul was telling the Ephesians here that salvation is not something they have to work hard to achieve. It is something that is there for the taking.

The story is told of a great painter who went to a certain town and saw on the street an old man dressed in old shabby rags. The famous artist approached the man and asked him if he would like to earn some money by posing for a painting. The old man agreed, and an appointment was made for the next day. At the appointed time, a knock came on the door. The artist opened to find a cleanly shaved and neatly dressed man standing at the door. "I've come as you requested," said the man. The artist looked at him and said, "Sir, the man I required for this painting was shabby and dirty; you are not that man." The artist wanted the man as he was with all his dirt and tattered clothes. This is just how the Lord wants you. Have you ever considered how much an insult it is to the Lord when we feel that we can get to heaven without him? To try to get to heaven by our own works is equal to saying, "Lord, I don't think I'll need your death on the cross. I think I can please God on my own."

Paul is very clear here. He is not saying, "Work hard and you will obtain the helmet of salvation." He simply says, "Take it."

Do you recall the story of Naaman in 2 Kings 5? He was a Syrian military commander who had the horrible disease of leprosy. His Israelite servant girl told him that the prophet Elisha could heal him of his disease. Excited about this possibility, he traveled to Israel to see Elisha. When Naaman arrived at Elisha's house, the prophet refused to come out of his house to greet him. Instead, Elisha told Naaman to go wash himself seven times in the Jordan River. Naaman was insulted: "'I thought that he would surely come out to me and stand and call on the name of the LORD his God, wave his hand over the spot and cure me of my leprosy. Are not . . . the rivers of Damascus, better than any of the waters of Israel? Couldn't I wash in them and be cleansed?' So he turned and went off in a rage." His servant, however, persuaded him to do just as the prophet had said. Naaman went to the Jordan (probably with great doubt and skepticism) and washed seven times. When he came out of the river the seventh time, he was healed. He was expecting to have to work hard for his healing. He was expecting great ceremony and pomp. His healing was there for the taking. All he had to do was take it. He almost refused because it seemed too simple.

How many people are like Naaman? They just cannot believe that salvation could be free and easy. Paul tells us here that all we have to do is take it. Jesus has done all the work. You don't have to do anything. You don't have to clean yourself up and live a better life first. Jesus asks you to come as you are. He will accept you, dirt and all. Salvation is simply a matter of receiving. "Take the helmet of salvation," wrote Paul. That is all there is to it. You don't have to wait any longer. You don't have to work harder. You don't have to clean yourself up more.

What is this salvation that Paul tells us to claim, and how does it protect us in the battle against the spiritual forces around us? First, let us understand that, by our very nature, we are sinners. As sinners, we are separated from God and under his wrath. No matter how hard we try, we cannot wipe away the stain of sin. Our good works and beliefs are merely flavor crystals we might add to a glass of poisoned water. We were indeed in a very delicate situation. Our lives were an offense to a holy God. We were under his judgment and wrath. Then Jesus came and took the punishment for our sins. He willingly died so that we could be forgiven.

How do you know if you have received this salvation? First, you will know because God is faithful to his word. Jesus tells us that if we believe in him, we will not be condemned (John 3:18). John 6:37 tells us that if we come to the Lord, he will not cast us out. These are the promises of a God who cannot lie. Take God at his word. Come to him now and place all your trust and confidence on him. You may or may not feel any great emotions, but don't be fooled by emotions. Salvation is a legal transaction between you and God. If you have already placed your trust in him and believe only in his work for your salvation, then take him at his word that he will never cast you out. He is more willing to offer this salvation than we are to receive it.

Second, you can know that you have the helmet of salvation because of the inner testimony of his Spirit in your life. Romans 8:16 tells us that the Spirit of God testifies to our spirit, assuring us that we are children of God. When you reach out to take the helmet of salvation, the Holy Spirit of God seals the relationship by coming to live in your heart. Your spiritual ears are opened to hear the voice of the Holy Spirit. He delights in giving you the assurance of your salvation. He delights in letting you know that you are truly God's child. You will experience that inner assurance in your own heart. It is the voice of God's Spirit within confirming your relationship with Christ and assuring you of your salvation.

Finally, you can be sure that you have taken the helmet of salvation because you will see evidence in your life. You will experience a change in your desires and ambitions. You will no longer delight in the things of the world in which you used to delight. You will begin to experience a deep hunger for the things of God. People around you will see the difference. You will be a new person. Jesus will live his life in you. What is important to note about all this is that these changes are not the result of your own effort to live a better life. These things are happening to you as the Holy Spirit of God changes you from the inside.

It should be noted here that this passage is addressed to Christians. In verse 10 Paul addressed them as brothers. Why should Paul tell those who have been saved to take this helmet of salvation when they already are saved? Perplexed about this, I took a late night stroll to ask the Lord about this. I happened to look up into the starlit sky. I was struck by the vastness of the universe in which we live. I was just a small speck in an infinite universe. As I stood there contemplating the vastness of it all, I believe God spoke to me and said, "Wayne, this is what my salvation is like. It is far more vast and much deeper than anything you have ever experienced." This was similar to the experience of Paul in Romans 11:33–35. Paul understood that the Lord was far bigger than anything he could ever experience.

Each day I live as a believer is a new day to claim afresh this wonderful salvation. Every day is an opportunity to draw deeper and deeper from this well. I take each day a new and fresh supply of forgiveness, righteousness, peace, and joy that are the result of this salvation in my life. Salvation also means a present deliverance from sin and a confident hope for a future of love and worship throughout all eternity. As I yield myself afresh each day to him who saved me from the slavery to sin, death, and eternal wrath, I experience more purity in thought, word, and deed. As I dig deeper and deeper and receive more and more of the fruit of this salvation in my life, I am more able to stand firm against the devil's charms.

In Philippians 3:12–14 Paul told the Philippians that he was still pressing on to take hold of the things of Christ. He strained toward the things that were ahead. He pressed on toward the goal. Paul told the Philippians to keep reaching forward. We will never drain God's well of forgiveness and peace. Our experience of this salvation will never be complete this side of glory. Eternity itself will not be sufficient to understand and experience everything there is in Christ.

There are many people who accept the Lord and think that they have arrived. They never mature in Christ's character. They remain babies in Christ and are prime targets of the enemy. Paul is telling us here that if we want to be protected, we need to take this helmet. We must draw deeply from this well of salvation each and every day. We need to allow this salvation of God to produce its fruit in us on a daily basis.

The helmet of salvation is foundational. Without it you are destined to an eternity without Christ. How important it is that you be sure of your salvation. Do you know that you are a child of God today? Not everyone is a child of God. Only those who by faith reach out and accept the payment for their sins offered them at the cross can know this salvation. Salvation involves a mental choice, as does putting on a helmet.

Have you reached out to the Lord Jesus? Does God's Spirit in you assure you of your place in the family of God? Do you see evidence of the person of Jesus living in you and delivering you from sin? Are you daily experiencing the present reality of this salvation in purity of thought, word, and deed? If you are not sure how to answer these questions, I challenge you to go to the Lord right now. Confess your sin and reach out to accept the helmet of salvation freely offered to all who will believe. Put that helmet on and wear it confidently. It is a symbol of your privileged status as a child of God.

For Consideration:

- Have you ever accepted the salvation that the Lord offers? How do you know? What evidence is there of this salvation in your life?

- How have you grown in your understanding of this salvation over the years? Is it more precious to you today than ever before?

- What fruit of this salvation have you experienced today?

- How does this salvation protect you from the attacks of the enemy?

For Prayer:

- Thank the Lord for the wonderful salvation he has offered to you.

- Ask him to give you a new daily appreciation of what the Lord Jesus has accomplished for your salvation.

- Take a moment to pray for a friend or relative who does not know this salvation of the Lord.

32

The Sword of the Spirit

Read Ephesians 6:17

The last of the pieces of armor is the sword of the Spirit. Paul tells us that this sword is the Word of God. Why is the Word of God called the "sword of the Spirit"? How does it help us in the battle before us? Let's consider these questions in some detail.

What is the "Word of God" spoken of here? The phrase "Word of God" in the Bible refers most often to the inspired Scriptures themselves (Isaiah 40:8; Mark 7:13). Paul also used this phrase, however, to refer to the preaching of the gospel (2 Corinthians 2:17; Philippians 1:14). We are safe in saying that the Bible itself and its teaching is the "word" that is being referred to here in this verse.

Why is the Word of God called the "sword of the Spirit"? We understand that the "Spirit" being referred to here is the Holy Spirit. The Bible is the "sword of the Holy Spirit" for two principle reasons.

First, he is the author of Scripture. This is the clear teaching of the apostle Peter in 2 Peter 1:20–21: "Above all, you must understand that no prophecy of Scripture came about by the prophet's own interpretation. For prophecy never had its origin in the will of man, but men spoke from God as they were carried along by the Holy Spirit." The Holy Spirit inspired the Scriptures that we have today in both the Old and New Testaments. He is their true author. It is for this reason that this "word" is attributed to him in this passage.

Second, the Word of God is called the sword of the Spirit because he chooses to use and empower it to accomplish the work of God in the lives of his people. John 17:17 tells us that we are sanctified (made like Christ) through the Word of God. Listen to what Paul tells us about the Scriptures in 2 Timothy 3:16–17: "All Scripture is God-breathed and is useful for teaching, rebuking, correcting and training in righteousness, so that the man of God may be thoroughly equipped for every good work." Paul tells us very clearly here that the Word of God has as its purpose to equip us in our life in Christ. It is the ministry of the Holy Spirit to apply Scripture to our lives. He breathes life into these words and plants them in our hearts to bring forth fruit. Without the work of the Holy Spirit, the words of Scripture do not have any deep spiritual impact on human lives.

In 1 Corinthians 2:14 we read: "The man without the Spirit does not accept the things that come from the Spirit of God, for they are foolishness to him, and he cannot understand them, because they are spiritually discerned." The only way we can truly understand the Scriptures is by means of the illumination of the Holy Spirit. God speaks directly to us as we read his holy book. It becomes life to us. We see its application to our everyday lives in ways we never saw before. The Scriptures are God's means of bringing us into maturity.

Paul, in writing to the Thessalonians, tells them in 1 Thessalonians 1:5: "Our gospel came to you not simply with words, but also with power, with the Holy Spirit and with deep conviction." Paul's preaching was not in words only but also in the power of the Holy Spirit. Very clearly it was the delight of the Holy Spirit to take the word he had inspired and empower its proclamation through the apostles. He still delights to do this today.

The sword of the Word of God empowered by the Holy Spirit is a very effective weapon against the forces of Satan. Maybe you can remember the time you came to know the Lord. Prior to this, you perhaps had read parts of the Bible but remained untouched. One day, however, you sat under the preaching of the gospel and were gripped by it. Your heart was broken, and tears streamed down your cheeks. It seemed that God was speaking directly to you through those words. You were experiencing the power that Paul spoke about in 1 Thessalonians 1:5. God's Word was so powerful that you could not resist it. It convicted you of your sin and set you free from the lies of Satan. That same gospel has changed countless lives in our world today.

Satan would have us lose sight of God's Word. His temptation of Eve in the garden of Eden centered around the word of God. He knew that if he could cause her to doubt the clear instructions of God, he would have her in his hands. Sometimes the only defense we have against the attack of the enemy is the clear teaching of Scripture. Jesus himself in his temptations held up the Word of God as his defense against Satan (see Matthew 4).

Be assured that Satan will do his best to cause you to doubt what God says. As never before, Satan has been causing our society to turn from the clear, inspired teachings of the Lord. Universities and seminaries that were founded on biblical doctrines have pushed them aside in favor of more modern ideals. God's Word has been pushed out of our schools. Churches across our nations are beginning to question its authority. Never before has the Christian community been so biblically illiterate. Our children are growing up knowing nothing of the teachings of Scripture.

Satan has been working very hard to discredit the authority and validity of the Bible in our day. The result has been a tidal wave of openly practiced immorality and confusion. This is fertile soil for Satan and his efforts. The church has lost her credibility in the community because she has, for the most part, abandoned the clear teaching of God's Word. We cannot afford to put down our sword. We need to put aside our own ideas and seek the clear guidance of Scripture. Like a compass, God's Word will guide us safely through the wilderness of confusion and lies that surround us.

Not only will Satan try to disprove this word, he will also try to misinterpret and misapply it. In the temptation of Jesus in Matthew 4, Satan did not hesitate to use Scripture to his own end. Is this not the reason for the success of the cults in our day?

Satan will also try to get us involved in disputes among ourselves over doctrines. It is hard to say whether his casting doubt on the Scripture or his misinterpreting it has caused more damage in the world today. On the one hand, we have the rise of secularism, which denies the authority of the Bible. On the other hand, we have radical divisions in the church caused by the misinterpretation of the Bible. What is clear in our society is that the enemy is doing his best to attack the sword of the Spirit. He knows how powerful a weapon it is in the hands of a true believer.

Let me say a few words about why God's Word is called a sword. It is a sword because of the judgment it brings. Ezekiel 21 speaks of a great sword that was going to be polished and sharpened to bring judgment on the earth. In Revelation 19:15 we read about the return of the Lord. He is described as having a great sword coming out of his mouth. That sword is a sword of judgment. One day each of us will be measured according to the standard of Scripture. It will not matter in the end what we think. God's Word will be our judge. It will also judge the demons of hell. Satan himself will stand before Jesus, the Word of God, and be condemned.

God's Word is also called a sword because it can pierce our hearts and discern our thoughts and intentions (Hebrews

4:12). Maybe you have experienced the power of this sword in your life. It brings conviction of sin. Like a light, it opens up the darkest secrets of our hearts. Like a surgeon's knife, it cuts away the unwanted sin and rebellion. It melts our resistance and challenges our attitudes. It is the delight of the Spirit of God to use his sword in your life to draw you closer to your Savior.

Another way in which God's Word is a sword is its ability to fend off the attacks of the enemy. It brings wisdom to us in our times of need. It comforts us in our discouragement. It brings peace to us in our confusion. With this Word we fend off the constant attacks of the enemy to discourage and confuse us. It becomes our assurance in times of doubt. It keeps us from falling into error.

The enemy cannot bear to see the fruit of this sword in our lives. He cringes as he sees it cut away the wrong attitudes he has worked so hard to cultivate. It grieves him when that sword penetrates deeply into the inner recesses of our lives to reveal hidden motives and secret sins. Satan is forced to flee at the point of this sword. He cannot resist it. One day that sword will turn on him for the last time. One word from the mouth of the Lord, one simple swipe of his sword, will bring Satan and his angels to their ultimate defeat.

How important the Word of God is today in the spiritual battle. Do you see it as a means of fending off the attacks of the enemy? Do you willingly place your life under the scrutiny of this sword? Are you willing to let it cut away the pieces of your life that do not bring glory to the Lord Jesus? Sometimes this is a painful process, but it is necessary if you are to defeat the enemy.

You cannot underestimate the power of the Word of God in the battle before you. Cling to it in your hour of temptation. Claim its promises when you are discouraged and downcast. Study it carefully when you are in need of understanding and wisdom. Trust it implicitly when you are in your moments of doubt. Speak it out with confidence and boldness. Search it daily for guidance and direction. The Word is a transforming sword. Its life-changing power can penetrate to the very heart of your being. This word alone has the power to counter the lies of the enemy. Hold tightly to it. Let nothing distract you from it. Victory can only be found in faithfulness to the Word of God.

For Consideration:

- Why is the Word of God called the sword of the Spirit?

- How has the Word of God been a defense for you against the attacks of the enemy? Give examples.

- Is there evidence around you that the enemy is attacking the Bible? What does this tell us about how important the sword of the Spirit is in our battle against the enemy?

- How much of a role does this sword play in your life today?

For Prayer:

- Thank God for the encouragement and blessing the Scriptures have been to you. Thank him that his Word has been your protection.

- Ask God to increase your hunger and thirst for his Word.

- Thank him for the power of this sword to transform life. Thank him that it will send the enemy into retreat.

33

Pray in the Spirit

Read Ephesians 6:18

S o far we have seen that the armor of the Christian has more to do with our position in Christ than what we do for him. In other words, victory in the battle before us does not so much depend on what we do but rather on who we are in Christ. If we want to win the battle before us, we must clothe ourselves with the character of Jesus Christ. This is one thing the enemy cannot tolerate. When he sees the character of Jesus being revealed in us, he must flee. If we want to defeat the enemy, we must clothe ourselves with what the Lord Jesus has done for us. Beyond this, however, there is something else Paul told the Ephesians they needed to do.

Pray on All Occasions

"Pray . . . on all occasions," said Paul. This is our role in the battle against Satan and his demons. Notice that he told the Ephesians to pray on "all occasions." We are not to pray only when things get difficult. However, that is often our practice. Many times it is only when we are backed into a corner and there seems to be no way out that we think of seeking the Lord's wisdom and power. Paul told the Ephesians that they needed to make prayer a way of life. They should not wait until Satan had attacked; instead, they should pray to prevent his attacks.

Paul is telling us that we are to bombard the forces of hell with constant prayer. Like the enemy's flaming arrows, these prayers penetrate the ranks of the demon army and break down the strongholds. Be assured that Satan will never stop his attack against the church. Day after day he persists in building up dividing walls. He does not let up in flinging the slime of bitterness and hatred. We cannot afford to let up in our prayers either. We must counter his arrows with our own. By prayer, the power of God is unleashed on the strongholds of Satan.

Do you remember the story of Moses' fight against the Amalekites in Exodus 17? These Amalekites battled relentlessly against the people of God to destroy them. During this time Moses stood on the top of a hill with his arms lifted high, holding the rod of God in his hands. As long as the hands of Moses were lifted up, the enemy suffered losses. When his hands grew tired and he let them down, the enemy began to win the battle. This is just how it is in the battle against Satan. Prayer wins the victory.

Paul challenged the Ephesians to be a people of prayer. Prayer must become our way of living. We must bathe our decisions in prayer. We must bathe our ministries in prayer. Prayer needs to become the central focus of the battle against Satan and his angels. The power of God is only released by means of prayer. Could it be that the reason Satan has been advancing so rapidly in our day is because we have lost sight of the need for prayer at all times and at all occasions? We do not need more human effort to fight Satan; we need more prayer. Scripture is filled with this principle. Consider the following examples:

- Then Jesus told his disciples a parable to show them that they should always pray and not give up. (Luke 18:1)

- Be joyful in hope, patient in affliction, faithful in prayer. (Romans 12:12)

- Do not be anxious about anything, but in everything, by prayer and petition, with thanksgiving, present your requests to God. (Philippians 4:6)

- Devote yourselves to prayer, being watchful and thankful. (Colossians 4:2)

- Pray continually. (1 Thessalonians 5:17)

It is quite easy to see just how important prayer is in this battle. If we are to win the battle before us, we are to be people who devote themselves to pray, at all times and in all occasions.

Pray with All Kinds of Prayers and Requests

Paul also told the Ephesians that they should pray all kinds of prayer. I would simply like to look at two types of prayer in this discussion: praise and intercession. First, regarding prayers of thanksgiving and praise, there are times when the enemy is defeated quickly by these kinds of prayers. When you feel him pressing in on you, lift up your voice in sincere praise and thanksgiving for the blessings the Lord has already given you. See what the result of this will be in the battle before you. When the enemy hears the sound of sincere praise, he retreats and you will feel immediately encouraged.

I can remember working in a church where the enemy had come in and caused great division. This particular church at one time had been a real witness to the community. But the blessing of God had been removed. It had been a long time since anyone had come to faith in Jesus; visitors sensed strife; believers could not get along. Bitterness and division permeated the entire work. During this time the Lord impressed on my heart the need for praise and thanksgiving in that work. I began to seek things for which we could praise the Lord as a church. Whenever we saw God work in the life of a member to respond in love and not in bitterness, we thanked the Lord. We began to focus on what God *was* doing, and things began to change. Soon we began to see more and more reasons to praise the Lord. It was not too long before the oppression began to lift. Satan could not tolerate the praise and thanksgiving. As long as he had God's people focused negatively on their problems, he was happy to stay. But he could not stay when their hearts began to be lifted up in praise. The strongholds of the enemy are broken by prayers of praise and thanksgiving.

A second form of prayer is supplication or intercessory prayer. In this type of prayer, we ask God to meet our needs or the needs of others. We need this type of prayer in the battle before us. God delights to give us what we need to face the battle before us. James 4:2 tells us that we do not have because we do not ask. Repeatedly in the Bible, we are called on to ask God for those things we need. Do you need wisdom to face the foe? Ask God. He promises to give it (James 1:5). Do you need strength or patience? Again it is there for the taking by prayer (1 Samuel 30:6). Everything we need to face the foe is there for us. All we need to do is ask. We have yet to see the power of prayer. Strongholds are brought down simply because we ask. The sick are healed according to God's will because we place them in his healing hands. The sinner is restored because someone prayed. Prayer taps us directly into the power of God. The enemy is powerless before this.

Pray in the Spirit

There is one final thing we need to look at in this verse. I have left this to the end because I want to underline its importance. Paul tells us here that we are to "pray in the Spirit." What does this phrase mean? The temptation in prayer is to come to the Lord with our own ideas. We tell God how he needs to work in the lives of our friends and relatives. We tell him how he is to run the universe and who he is to heal. This is not the type of prayer Paul was speaking about here. He was not advocating a "name it, claim it" mentality in prayer.

When Paul tells us that we are to pray in the Spirit, I believe he is telling us that we need to pray according to the leading and under the direction and inspiration of the Spirit. This type of prayer is only possible when we are in tune with the prompting of God's Holy Spirit and the clear teaching of Scripture. Listen to what R.A. Torrey says about praying in the Spirit:

> When we come into God's presence, we should recognize our infirmity, our ignorance of what is best for us, our ignorance of what we should pray for, our ignorance of how we should pray for it, and, in the consciousness of our utter inability to pray aright, we should look up to the Holy Spirit to teach us to pray aright, and cast ourselves utterly upon Him to direct our prayer and to lead out our desires and guide our utterance of them. There is no place where we need to recognize our ignorance more than in prayer. Rushing heedlessly into God's presence and asking the first thing that comes into our minds, or that some other thoughtless person has asked us to pray for is not praying in the Holy Spirit and is not true prayer. We must wait for the Holy Spirit and surrender ourselves to the Holy Spirit. The prayer that God the Holy Spirit inspires is the prayer that God the Father answers. (R.A. Torrey, *The Person and Work of the Holy Spirit* (Grand Rapids: Zondervan, 1974), 131–132)

I believe that Torrey is right. How often have we thoughtlessly rushed into prayer, praying for this and that with no thought of what God's will might be? Paul is telling us that we need to pray according to the leading and prompting of the Holy Spirit. Satan does not need to worry about the prayers we pray in the flesh, seeking our own will. He may even encourage us to continue to pray selfishly. James spoke about this type of prayer in James 4:3 when he said: "When you ask, you do not receive, because you ask with wrong motives, that you may spend what you get on your own pleasures."

Satan is more than happy to keep us praying in the flesh,

because then we are no threat to him. Eventually, we will become discouraged and lose heart. How different, however, are those prayers inspired by the Holy Spirit himself. These prayers are filled with power. These prayers send the forces of hell into retreat. Satan cannot resist those who pray in the Spirit's leading.

Prayer is far more than telling God how we think he should run the universe. True prayer is Spirit inspired. God will answer these prayers because they are according to his will. The apostle John makes this abundantly clear in 1 John 5:14–15: "This is the confidence we have in approaching God: that if we ask anything according to his will, he hears us. And if we know that he hears us—whatever we ask—we know that we have what we asked of him."

Only by understanding the Word of God and knowing the prompting of the Spirit of God can we ask for those things that are according to the will of God. True prayer can only happen when I am in communion with God's Holy Spirit. If we are open to his leading, the Holy Spirit will lead us in how to pray. He will direct us in what we need to pray. He will even pray for us and enable us to pray well (Romans 8:26). Pray at every opportunity those prayers that are motivated and inspired by the Holy Spirit of God. This type of prayer is very powerful and will send the enemy into quick retreat.

For Consideration:

• When should we pray?

• What is the difference between praying in the flesh and praying in the Spirit?

• What is it about prayer that makes it such a powerful force against the attacks of the enemy?

• What is God telling you through this passage about your own personal prayer life?

For Prayer:

- Thank God for the privilege of prayer and how he chooses to work through your prayers to accomplish his wonderful purposes.

- Ask God to help you in your life of prayer. Ask him to teach you how to pray as his Spirit directs.

34

Be Alert

Read Ephesians 6:18

In this meditation we will conclude our reflection on the armor of God with two final comments related to the spiritual battle before us.

Be Alert

The first thing Paul told the Ephesians here is that they were to be alert. Let us remember the context of this passage. Paul had been trying to communicate that we are involved in a great spiritual battle. Many of us live our lives with no thought of this battle before us. Let me assure you that the battle is very much on the mind of Satan. This is his passion and obsession. His whole focus is to destroy the work of God. He and his angels are right now working as hard as they can to distract and destroy the work that God wants to do in your life. You dare not deny this battle. To do so is to deny the authority of the Scriptures themselves. The apostle Peter stated it this way in 1 Peter 5:8: "Be self-controlled and alert. Your enemy the devil prowls around like a roaring lion looking for someone to devour."

You can be sure that you are on Satan's hit list. He is watching your every move. He is waiting for the right moment to send his flaming arrow in your direction. You may hear him whisper in your ear. You may feel him rile your spirit. When you least expect it, he will come rushing straight at you with his bag of temptations. What Paul was telling the Ephesians here is that they needed to live their lives in the knowledge of the battle before them. They were to be alert.

The Greek word for "alert" can also be translated as "keep awake." Listen to what the Lord told the church of Sardis in Revelation 3:2–3: "Wake up! Strengthen what remains and is about to die, for I have not found your deeds complete in the sight of my God. Remember, therefore, what you have received and heard; obey it, and repent. But if you do not wake up, I will come like a thief, and you will not know at what time I will come to you."

Through his servant John, the Lord Jesus pleaded with his people to wake up. Notice here that if they didn't wake up, they would die. The sleep of God's people here was not an innocent sleep. It was the sleep of death. As they slept, Satan drained them of all their spiritual vitality. If they did not wake up, they would perish. Jesus told them here that their sleep was sin. They needed to repent.

I wonder if these are not words for the church of our day. Have we been guilty of falling asleep while the enemy ravages our society? We have seen whole churches that are consumed by bitterness and jealousy fall into the hands of the enemy. We have seen whole denominations turn their backs on the clear and authoritative teaching of the Word of God. We have watched believers become absorbed in tradition and denominationalism and lose all sense of perspective in their faith. We have been thoroughly frustrated by those who seem to be content to remain stagnant in their spiritual walk, showing no signs of spiritual growth from year to year. We are seeing immorality glamorized on our televisions, in our "top of the chart" hit songs, and in our best-selling books. Years from now, future generations may very well ask, "Where were the believers when all this was happening?" Have we fallen asleep? This is by no means an innocent sleep. As we sleep, the enemy is sucking the life out of our churches and society. This is a sleep of death.

The call to wake up is very real. In Romans 13:11 Paul wrote: "And do this, understanding the present time. The hour has come for you to wake up from your slumber, because our salvation is nearer now than when we first believed." As the days of the end approach, we will need to be even more vigilant. Satan will redouble his efforts. We cannot afford to sleep because this is the hour of battle.

In 2 Kings 6 we have a very interesting story about the prophet Elisha and his servant. The enemy king of Syria was trying to capture the prophet of God and had surrounded the city where Elisha was staying. When his servant looked out and saw the city surrounded by the enemy, he feared for his life. Elisha prayed to God to open the eyes of his servant so he could really see what was out there. When God opened the servant's eyes, the servant saw the mountains filled with horses and chariots of fire. These were the angels of God sent to protect Elisha and his servant. I have often wondered what it would be like to see for an instant the unseen spiritual battle that rages around us. I don't believe that we would ever be the same again. Unseen to the naked eye, the battle rages. We dare not sleep.

Pray for All the Saints

There is a second thing we need to understand from this passage. Paul told the Ephesians that, in light of the battle before them, they needed to be always praying for the saints. This tells me something very important. In this battle we need to be watching out for each other.

In this particular context, Paul challenged the Ephesians to pray for him that he would be given great boldness in the gospel. The Lord expects us to stand behind his servants in the proclamation of the gospel. By our prayers we wrestle alongside our brothers and sisters in the cause of Christ.

In Galatians 6 Paul told the Galatians that they were to

watch out for each other in the battle before them. He told them that if they saw a brother who was overtaken in a particular sin, they were to do their part to restore him in a spirit of gentleness. Paul also told the Galatians that they were to bear each other's burdens. The Galatians were to take every opportunity to do good to their brothers and sisters in the faith. No one should have to fight the battle alone. As a family, we are to look out for each other.

What a wonderful thing it is to know that I have a team of prayer warriors to cover me as I rush forward to attack the forces of hell. It was never God's intent that we fight this battle on our own. He has promised to clothe us with all the necessary armor. By prayer we bombard the devil's strongholds. Together as one mighty army we watch out for and support each other in this great battle against the foe. With our armor in place, prayer as our weapon, and our brothers and sisters beside us, we advance in the name of Christ. In him we are more than conquerors.

For Consideration:

- What evidence is there around us (in our church and society) of the presence of the enemy?

- Have you been alert? Are there any areas where your society or your church is sleeping?

- Do you have prayer covering your ministry? How important is this covering?

- Are you supporting your brothers and sisters in prayer? Are there people that you need to be more diligently praying for?

For Prayer:

- Ask God to make you more aware of the nature of the battle around you today.

- Ask the Lord to help you to be more alert and to take this battle seriously.

- Ask him to show you what you need to do to awaken others to the reality of the spiritual warfare.

- Take a moment to pray for a friend who is struggling today.

35

Concluding Comments

Read Ephesians 6:19–24

Paul had challenged the believers in Ephesus to pray in the Spirit on all occasions. Here in verses 19 and 20, he asked them for particular prayer for himself and the ministry to which the Lord had called him. He asked them to pray specifically that the Lord would help him to speak fearlessly. There are a few things that need to be mentioned here about this request of Paul.

Notice first that Paul was not depending on his own wisdom to proclaim the mysteries of God. He asked the Ephesians to pray that whenever he opened his mouth, words would be given him. These were not his words but were words inspired by the Holy Spirit. In 1 Corinthians 2 Paul reminded the Corinthians that when he came to them, he made up his mind not to preach his own wisdom among them. Of all the apostles, Paul was probably the most educated. It would have been extremely easy for him to trust his own education and knowledge to convince people. Paul's prayer was that the Lord would keep him from this.

Notice second that Paul struggled with fear. We often see the apostle as a man who knew no fear. When he wrote to the Corinthians, however, he told them that when he came to them, he came in weakness, fear, and trembling (1 Corinthians 2:3). The apostle had every human reason to be afraid. His life was at stake at every moment. When he spoke in the name of the Lord, he often infuriated his audiences. Paul knew that his message would not always be accepted. He needed boldness to speak the words that God gave him. The ministry of speaking the mysteries of God was not for cowards. Paul was God's ambassador in chains. Speaking the words of the Lord Jesus had put this great apostle in prison.

Notice finally in these verses that the apostle needed to be willing to open his mouth. He did not wait until some bolt of lightening stuck him. God generally does not force us to speak in his name. On the contrary, when we willingly surrender our lips to him, he uses us. He is gentle in nature. As Paul opened his mouth, God used it. If he had stayed home waiting for God to open his mouth for him, he would never have accomplished the things he did for the glory of God. Each time the apostle opened his mouth was an act of faith. He needed to trust that the Lord would fill his mouth with the right words.

God expects us to take a stand also. He expects us to move forward in faith. When you pray that God would give you words, you need to open your mouth to speak. When you pray that God would give you contact with unbelievers, you need to move forward in faith and reach out to those right around you. It is no good to pray if you are not willing to step out in faith.

Paul concluded his letter with a few comments about his friend Tychicus, who had traveled with Paul on his missionary journey (Acts 20:4). Obviously restricted in his movements, the apostle sent Tychicus to the Ephesians to let them know how he was doing and also to encourage them in their faith. Could it be that Tychicus was the one to deliver this letter to the Ephesians? No doubt Tychicus would return to the apostle Paul with news about the Ephesians as well.

As the apostle concluded his letter, he blessed the Ephesian church with the peace, love, faith, and grace from God the Father and the Lord Jesus Christ. His desire for the Ephesians was that the abundance of the Lord Jesus would be their portion. By grace God had created the church and equipped it to live in a unified community and wage a victorious war against all the forces of evil. The knowledge and practice of the things contained in this book would keep the Ephesian believers through all the struggles and trials they would face. May we too grow into the fullness of Christ in us to the praise of God the Father.

For Consideration:

- What does this passage teach us about how important prayer was to the apostle Paul?

- What causes you to fear speaking out in the name of the Lord?

- What is the relationship between opening our mouths and letting God fill them? Why do you suppose God does not force us to do his will?

For Prayer:

- Ask the Lord to give you the boldness you need to speak his word.

- Ask the Lord to give you a deeper experience of his grace, love, and peace.

- Thank him for times when he specifically empowered you to speak in his name.

Light To My Path
Devotional Commentary Series

A new commentary series
for every day devotional use.

Other books available from Authentic

Authentic

129 Mobilization Drive
Waynesboro, GA 30830

706-554-1594
1-8MORE-BOOKS
ordersusa@stl.org
www.authenticbooks.com

An Introduction To The New Testament
Three Volume Collection

D. Edmond Hiebert

Though not a commentary, *An Introduction to the New Testament* presents each book's message along with a discussion of such questions as authorship, composition, historical circumstances of their writing, issues of criticism and provides helpful, general information on their content and nature. The bibliographies and annotated book list are extremely helpful for pastors, teachers, and laymen as an excellent invitation to further careful exploration.

This book will be prized by all who have a desire to delve deeply into the New Testament writings.

> Volume 1: The Gospels and Acts
> Volume 2: The Pauline Epistles
> Volume 3: The Non-Pauline Epistles and Revelation

1-884543-74-X   976 Pages

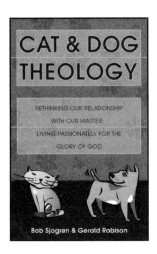

Cat and Dog Theology
Rethinking Our Relationship With Our Master

Bob Sjogren & Dr. Gerald Robison

There is a joke about cats and dogs that conveys their differences perfectly.

A dog says, "You pet me, you feed me, you shelter me, you love me, you must be God."

A cat says, "You pet me, you feed me, you shelter me, you love me, I must be God."

These God-given traits of cats ("You exist to serve me") and dogs ("I exist to serve you") are often similar to the theological attitudes we have in our view of God and our relationship to Him. Using the differences between cats and dogs in a light-handed manner, the authors compel us to challenge our thinking in deep and profound ways. As you are drawn toward God and the desire to reflect His glory in your life, you will worship, view missions, and pray in a whole new way. This life-changing book will give you a new perspective and vision for God as you delight in the God who delights in you.

1-884543-17-0   224 Pages